Around Britain in 80 Days

by

Richard Digance

A nostalgic journey around Britain's coastline

About The Author

Richard Digance is a BAFTA Nominated entertainer and a proud recipient of The Gold Award from The British Academy of Composers and Songwriters. He is also one of just a handful of folksinger/songwriters listed in The Virgin Anthology of Songwriters.

He has spent most of his adult life travelling the country following his musical profession, performing over 4,000 concerts, recording 43 albums and publishing 21 books. He knows most of Britain like the back of his hand, but now is the time to hug the coastline, all of it, and travel to parts of Britain that conjure up special memories of past visits with the additional bonus of areas he has never visited before.

Born in West Ham, London, in 1949, he went to college in Glasgow before returning home, inspired by the folk music he heard when attending the college folk club at The Rockfield Hotel in Paisley.

His TV career spanned 17 years, culminating with his own ITV show for London Weekend Television, on which he played a guitar duet with Queen's Brian May, as well as playing with Status Quo and The Moody Blues. He also appeared on Channel 4s Countdown nearly 200 times.

On the comedy front he supported movie legend Steve Martin in America and Robin Williams at The London Palladium, the world-famous theatre where he also supported Roy Orbison and even tuned the legend's sacred red guitar.

His children's book, The Animal Alphabet, serialised by The BBC, is still used around the world in 15 different countries as an English teaching aid.

Richard now lives a quieter life in the Wiltshire countryside, allowing him to reflect on great memories from a life well lived. It is those memories that allow him to travel around Britain and take you with him as he does so. Most places in Britain hide a theatrical or musical memory for him and, together, we will share such memories.

This book is dedicated to anyone and everyone who has seen
me perform anywhere at any time in Britain.
I do not know most of you but this book is for you.
I thank you for your support.

The Introduction

Before you compare my work to someone else, a certain best-selling author by the name of Bill Bryson, I would suggest that he isn't the only person who travels Britain and writes about it. I have been doing exactly that for 54 years now and so I've probably been round the country more times than Mr Bryson has opened his laptop. Not exactly true of course, but you know what I mean.

At the outset, this book seems to be nothing different to the subject matter that the great man hasn't already written about, the travelling around a nation and noting its idiosyncrasies, but hey, please stop there, my adventure is nothing like that at all. Bill visits, observes and discovers whereas I'm re-visiting and re-discovering as I plunge deep into my memory bank that goes back half a century and that's a hell of a difference.

Many of the experiences mentioned within these pages are not researched as they come from my personal memories, but then again, in complete contradiction there are historical documents dating back to Roman times that I looked up and read about. After all, it wasn't too long after the Romans left that I turned up and went on the road, well it does seem that long ago to me anyway, so these are my very own memories and, my very own recollections of previous trips re-lived as I drive around Britain's rocks and beaches.

The historical facts told to me on past journeys by locals were mostly stored away in my grey matter from the last time I was in any given part of Britain. On many occasions, as the memories came flooding back, I saw the faces of those who were part of any given special moment. The rare times I visited locations new to me I used tourist information. So, now you see it's quite the opposite to Bill Bryson's tales.

I feel honoured to have worked with Bill Bryson, composing audiobook music and songs for him and I love his work so it was the most pleasurable of experiences, but here I blaze my own, very different trail to Bill's. There is another huge difference in as much as I have no intention of going inland like he has done many times, this being a journey around Britain's coastline and only Britain's coastline, something I've always wanted to do in a VW camper van, just like I did when I started out. All that said, if you still choose to compare me with Bill Bryson, an impeccable writer, then please be my guest as I will consider such comparisons an honour.

I suppose it seems strange that after so many years on the road as a musician I feel excited to be taking on, yes, a fairly gruelling journey in my chosen vehicle as a kind of excursion of leisure and pleasure.

So now the time has finally come to check the oil, spark plugs and tyre pressures and get on out there in an old banger that might not even make it. I admit to feeling very much the same but I'm about to give it a good go. An old bloke in an old camper van, what can possibly go wrong?

There is an additional factor to my plan. As a youngster I watched a film, yes the word movie only applied to American films back then, called Around The World In 80 Days, based on the classic book by Jules Verne. He was French, as were my ancestors who came to Britain in 1763, so maybe I felt some kind of a connection, maybe I didn't. He wrote the book in 1872 when travel was slightly different to today, hang on, not slightly different but completely different, after all, there were no motorway closures, diversions, rip-off Services or average speed limits to contend with in this modern world. In contrast, in 1872, if you wanted to go anywhere you simply went about your business with no questions asked, often on a horse-drawn carriage, a mode of transport not used anymore judging by the lack of water-troughs and bales of hay at petrol stations. There was a time in September 2021 when it was difficult to even find fuel, let alone searching refreshments and facilities for your horse.

Vernes told the story of Phileas Fogg, a chancer of a Londoner like myself, and Jean, whose surname I can't recall, his French man-in-waiting, who took on a bet that they could, or maybe couldn't, circumnavigate the world in 80 days. The wager was £20,000, the equivalent of nearly £2 million today. Half a century later they adapted the book into a film, released in 1956, which starred the inimitable David Niven and Shirley MacLaine and I well remember watching it as a youngster with a fair number of giggles. They sail, they float in a balloon and travel overland to win the bet. There was memorable music too. Well, perhaps not that memorable, but I just happen to remember some of it, not quite the same thing. I don't have a yacht and I don't have a head for heights so my journey will be far different to theirs, and substantially shorter in miles I hope, although, whatever the outcome the number of days will remain exactly the same.

So, loosely based on such an adventure I have decided to take to the highways and byways of Britain and drive around its perimeter, never, like Bill Bryson, going inland or like Jules

Vernes, taking to the air, either. It would be a distance of around 6,000 miles, or so I thought, which I would cover in the same 80 days as Vernes, driving, approximately, 75 or 80 miles per day, or so I thought again. Ha, it seemed a reasonable target when I planned the journey back in Salisbury during the enforced lockdown that put paid to exactly what I'm about do if that makes sense.

To get it all into some kind of perspective, the journey I am undertaking is double the distance from Britain to The United States of America, which by plane would take just 7 hours with someone else doing the arduous task of driving. This trip may be slightly more exhausting but, on the plus side, I trust the food will be more enjoyable.

Needless to say, it wouldn't be an impossible task by any means. Indeed, anyone with a Satnav and a driving licence could have taken on the very same challenge, but my attempt would, hopefully, offer something little bit different. For starters, I had no intention of using a Satnav with an irate woman bellowing the shortest route every five minutes, quite the opposite, as my task involved intentionally taking the longest route in most instances and enjoying the stunning scenery on offer. My Satnav woman would never understand and she'd lose her short-fused temper after the first hour, so she isn't invited. Please understand it's not my intention to be sexist here, I'm sure there are male Satnav presenters too, but it's just that I have never heard any.

We all have books that sit on a shelf, never opened, and such is the case with my road atlas. It's been covered in cobwebs for years. Like the recipe books in my kitchen it hasn't seen the light of day for a very long times, many of them probably going back to the days when Delia Smith ruled the roost and Jamie Oliver was still eating baby rusks.

Having been on the road for over half a century as a musician I have already been to most parts of Britain, sadly not including Ireland where I only ever did one gig. For geographical reasons I sadly cannot include Northern Ireland on my journey as it has no continuous coastline once it collides with the Irish Republic on its western and eastern outposts. Its coastline is like a giant horseshoe ending at two cul-de sacs either side. It's a shame because I love Ireland, its people and definitely the inspiring music they play. Maybe I'll do Northern Ireland another time as I'd really love to explore its small villages with pubs filled with wonderful music. On second thoughts I have a funny feeling I'd find an atmospheric music pub, close the road atlas, and stay there for the whole 80 days. Yes, it actually hurts to realise I can't add beautiful Ireland to my coastline journey and I send my apologies to my friends over there.

When my life on the road began in the late 1960s I owned a VW camper van, HTW 177H, a loveable cream object that never exceeded the speed limit because it couldn't. Many years have passed since then but my nostalgic, dream-come-true journey around Britain in 80 days would be done in the very same vehicle. Motor homes are exotic contraptions these days, but I wanted to include the pioneering romance of the old VW in my story. A bed, a sink and an engine at the back like a speedboat. Back on the road again, my VW is so old it has an outside toilet and I'm now so old too I will probably need that outside toilet more frequently than I used to.

And so begins the journey as the memories begin to flow, fifty years of driving to gigs, often not staying long enough to take in a place and its history, something I wish to amend here. Rarely did I travel the coastal roads as I am now about to do, always taking the most direct overland route to a theatre, and so it would be an enlightening experience for me as much as my readers as I re-visit places from a different direction with a different perspective, although many theatres I have played shall be mentioned as that's what this is all about. Off the top of my head I think there will be around 200 of them, 300 if I include the clubs I played too.

Time now to climb aboard the trusty VW camper van as I make my way down the busy A36 from Salisbury, the city in the countryside, where I now live, 18 miles to the south coast of England where our 80-day journey around Britain begins. Have I packed everything? To be honest there wasn't much to pack as I'm not entering any posh establishments. I've decided to take a similar wardrobe to what I took over 50 years ago, jeans, tee-shirts and a baseball cap in case the sin-visor snaps on route.

Can you possibly imagine 80 days without a mobile phone or social media? Bliss. Not a single text, selfie or scenic photo in sight. This is all about my memory getting to work and not some modern-day invention. There is bound to be some wonderful moments but they can be stored away in my head and within these pages only, making such a pleasant change from the obvious. I hope you agree.

One of Britain's greatest poets, John Betjeman, wrote about 'all along the south coast' but, just like Bill Bryson, I'm doing it in a far different way to Betjeman who wrote of deckchairs and men who wore knotted handkerchiefs for hats. No, this is not going to be a literary version of a picture postcard from the seaside.

I'm not saying for one minute the estimated mileage is correct, by the way, as 6,000 miles does seem an awfully long way to drive, a tad extreme maybe, and just thinking about it, who was the clever person who walked around our island with a tape-measure anyway? No doubt we shall discover its accuracy as we make our way round in the next 11 weeks or so.

The actual mileage is completely irrelevant anyway, so I'm not too concerned. The only thing that matters is that the next 80 days are fun, just like the last 50 years have been.

So here we go, fasten your seatbelts and happy travelling.

Day 1

Heading towards the south coast of England we stare at The English Channel as we enter the chaos of Southampton. Obviously, Southampton has been the starting point for many journeys including The Titanic, not a particularly successful excursion it has to be said, along with numerous world cruises. Those cruise ships are certainly brave objects having heard of the Titanic's outcome in 1912, but still they go and, luckily for all concerned, they all manage to get back again. In my case, if the VW engine blows up it won't be a case of women and children first.

Brave soldiers sailed to war via Southampton and the lucky ones returned to the same port, me being one when we came back safe and sound from The Falklands in the 1980s. Now it's my turn to do it again, although not by sea this time but by the A36 and the M271, the only motorway I shall encounter for a few months as once the trek begins from my Southampton base then motorways shall be forbidden. Actually, let's say our turn rather than my turn to do it again because I would like to invite you to come along with me and share my adventures first-hand.

So hello and goodbye Southampton for starters. When I first played Southampton's Mayflower Theatre, with Steeleye Span, it was actually Southampton Gaumont, it was that long ago, with the defunct Polygon Hotel opposite, and so it doesn't take me long to realise the changes I will encounter in the next 80 days if Southampton is anything to go by. The Polygon? Sadly, Pol has indeed gone. Only 20 minutes into the 80 days and I'm already reminiscing. I sense that's the way it's going to be. So many musical venues to pass in Southampton, from The Mayflower to The Cutty Wren, from The Brook to Hanger Farm Arts Centre and The Concorde Club in Eastleigh for whom I wrote their Christmas Pantomime. As a sign of things to come, I must have done over 50 gigs in Southampton through the years and it will be much the same in other towns and cities too.

Heading south we have a choice of turning left in the van and heading for Sussex or right towards The West Country via Dorset. I decide to turn left, keeping the dreaded M27 above me as I cross the Itchen Bridge and hug the coast, saving the glorious cream teas and clotted cream of The West Country for the final stage of our journey in a few months' time. In other words, we are going around Britain in an anti-clockwise direction. No, you're not sitting in the passenger seat, I get that, but I'd love you to join me in spirit, so, you kind of are. Who was it who said nostalgia was a thing of the past? Well, it certainly wasn't me. I'm so old now I remember when there was no such thing as history, just current affairs.

It's an appropriate beginning to my long journey, passing through Southampton to the naval bastion of Portsmouth, home of The Railway Hotel where I performed many times, close to where some absent-minded captain wrote off The Mary Rose, as we then drive the 55 miles to Chichester, where the Digances settled when they escaped from the Huguenot persecution in France.

I smile as I recall the time I played Chichester folk club to an audience of zero, made funnier by the fact the club organiser cancelled the raffle which I would undoubtedly have won under the circumstances. I've paid my respects to Arundel Cricket Club that used to have a very friendly folk club and I

13

eventually park the van on the promenade outside Worthing Pavilion, a venue I played many times too. I laughed out loud just now. I remember the old stage doorman, Arthur, telling me how they'd just had a dreadful show starring a faith healer. In his own words; 'Honestly, Richard, he was so bad a man in a wheelchair got up and walked out.'

Onwards and eastwards, around the one-way system of Brighton where I filmed my only DVD at The Dome, we see The Royal Pavilion to our right. It's the most out of place building in Britain in my opinion, looking more like something shipped over from India on the back of a giant trailer than a building that they began in 1787 and completed halfway through the next century. It was built for King George 1V, obviously with a little help from his friends, and it remained in royal hands until Queen Victoria sold it, if they wanted it or not, to the city of Brighton in 1850. The oversized Airfix kit of strange Raj shape. I spend my first night in the carpark of The Stamford Arms, an old Charringtons pub at Preston Circus with a small function room that housed Brighton Folk Club.

Brighton is my first real reminder of how I started out and how I built my career, or at least tried to. There's the room in the pub before pa systems were used, where I played to a capacity audience of 75, and then The Dome where I sold out the 1,700 seats in 1985. There's now a massive Conference Centre too, where I plied my trade as a corporate event entertainer. It was all there, my own personal history, all in one city. I should add here that Brighton wasn't even a city, but a town when I took the VW camper van there for the first time. It wasn't granted city status until 2001, round about 30 years after I began my life on the road. This is my first taste of how much things have changed over the years since I began. It's so comforting for me to look in the rear-view mirror to see that I haven't changed a bit since my career began. Leave it.

Day 2

Speaking of history, which I suppose we were when you think I began my life on the road in the late 1960s, we're on our way to Hastings, a distance of approaching 40 miles, where something rather riotous occurred in 1066. Actually, it didn't. The famous Battle of Hastings didn't happen in Hastings at all just in case you didn't know.

My drive along the A27 towards Hastings sees me pass Newhaven and on to Eastbourne where my second play, Fear of Frying, began its British tour at The Congress Theatre. Eastbourne, like so many other outpost towns, is a kind of cul-de-sac on the coast whereby you drop south of the A27 to get in before driving out again on the A259 towards Pevensey Bay, a popular haunt of William The Conqueror. To think he used the same by-pass as me. We are still 17 miles from Hastings and somewhere between here and Bexhill is where the famous battle really took place. To set the record straight, this is where William landed with his blood-thirsty gang on 28th September 1066 as a starting line for what we all learnt in school as The Norman Conquest, but the battle didn't happen until a few weeks later, 7 miles north-west of Hastings on 14th October. Just so you know. Just outside Hastings is the town of Battle, which may well serve as some kind of clue.

Driving along the once mighty promenade of once mighty white buildings I reach The White Rock Theatre, opposite the pier before heading east out of the town towards Fairlight Cove, a steep climb towards Hastings Folk Club for many years. I played both a good few times.

Bear in mind my trusty VW camper van isn't exactly the fastest of vehicles, I feel I tested it enough yesterday, during Day 1. Also considering the long journey ahead over the next 78 days I reckon Fairlight is a beautiful spot to bed down for the night and so it shall be done. It's quite windy in this part of the country, rushing in from The English Channel, just like Bill The Conqueror did. This kind of weather probably explains why King Harold managed to get something in his eye. I'm not surprised. It could have been an irritating speck of sand but, unfortunately for Harold, it was an arrow.

Day 3

Today I intent to complete my journey through East Sussex and onwards to Kent in a giant anticlockwise arc, ending up in Margate, home of the huge Winter Gardens that oozed afternoon teas whilst listening to a string quartet a century or so ago back in Victorian England. Those were the days of proper England when proper people drank proper tea from a teapot. Now come on, when was the last time you saw a tea-strainer? Yes, a tea-strainer, a round thing with holes in.

With Sussex in our rear-view mirror we continue further on our way, keeping to the coast road, towards the sanity of the Kent countryside. Now when I say sanity I exclude the stupidly small Romney, Hythe and Dymchurch Railway, a 13-mile, 15-inch gauge track that ends at the forbidding looking Dungeness power station where passengers dismount with violent cramp.

As a Vicarage Lane, East Ham schoolboy I holidayed here, staying in a deserted army Nissan hut beside the St Mary's Bay railway station. There was sod all to do on that holiday other than travel on the very same railway every day with my classmates. Yes, I accept that people were smaller years ago, but I don't believe they were that small in 1927 when it went into service. Even Snow White's chums would have been a little on the large side, grammatically incorrect I think, a little on the large side, and would have felt the discomfort. I still remember Hercules, a bright red engine the height of a kitchen sink. It belongs more in a Thomas The Tank Engine book than in a real-life scenario, pulling little passengers like me along with our knees wrapped around our chins as we pretended to enjoy the ride. Strangely though, I really did enjoy the ride and I still remember how much I really loved that school holiday, along with the train rides, but I can't for the life of me think why, but it was over 60 years ago.

There's a quaint parking area between St Mary's Bay and the sea and that will do me fine as a place to get my head down. Three days completed and everything is going exactly to plan. Tomorrow I drive northwest, beyond Deal, Sandwich and Ramsgate to the edge of Kent where Margate hangs on to the rest of England for grim death.

I need to take in Dover on route as the Town Hall was an occasional venue, mainly remembered for feeling important by getting changed in the mayor's chambers and it's also the nearest I shall come on this long journey to visiting another country. France, my family's homeland, is only 24 miles away to the east and you can almost smell the garlic wafting across the sea. This is the very spot where people cover themselves in goose-fat, like some Christmas dinner, and swim The Channel, encountering a few jellyfish as they do so for pudding. Hey, they're only swimming a width when you think about it, something that most of us did at school to win a ribbon that mum stitched on our trunks, so it's no big deal. Swimming a length of The Channel would be far more impressive.

Matthew Webb was the first pompous chap to swim The Channel to Calais in 1875. It took him 22 hours no less. Yes, of course a ferry would have cost him a few bob but surely it would have saved him time and trouble. Not content with that, 8 years later he then tried to swim The Whirlpool Rapids at the bottom of Niagara Falls, something considered totally impossible. It was totally impossible and he drowned. He jumped off a rowing boat near The Niagara Falls Suspension Bridge and ended up in Oakwood Cemetery, New York. I have no desire to have a swim today so best I make my way on to Margate with a folksong ringing in my head, A Shropshire Lad, written by the aforementioned John Betjeman, a song I often heard sung in the folk clubs by my mate John Kirkpatrick.

Day 4

Day 4 begins bright and early. Speaking of holiday resorts, East End of London folk, back in the day, went to Margate for a break after hop-picking working holidays in what they called the Garden of England, long before my old mates Chas and Dave made a few quid singing about the place. I continue to make my way there, waving a hello to The Spa Pavilion in Folkestone as I pass, a theatre built precariously on the side of a cliff, quite literally. On a clear day you can see France from the dressing-room window so I always said that Folkestone was the nearest I ever came to being an international artist. The entrance to The Channel Tunnel is here too but I have no intention of making a diversion to France as it wouldn't seem right after my ancestors had sacrificed so much to get away from there in the first place. I don't have too much time for the French because they don't speak English like me. They seem to have a different word for everything and I think that's rude.

Once in Margate, it's worth stopping off to visit The Turner Contemporary Art Gallery that I have recently read about. I should really as it cost them £15 million to build the place even though Turner was a bit of a misery if the film of his life was correct. By all accounts he climbed to the top of a ship's mast during a violent storm to feel the energy and atmospherics of the sky that he became so famous for painting. Bit over the top maybe but it obviously worked. It makes you wonder what he did to all the female models he painted, maybe he climbed on top of them too, a far more sensible and rewarding plan in my book.

In more recent times I performed at The Tom Thumb Theatre on the B2051 in the Cliftonville area east of Margate, a venue that boasts to being one the smallest theatres in the world. If you can't sell this place out you may as well throw in the towel, even if it isn't big enough to throw a towel anywhere. Its bright red exterior isn't much bigger than an equally bright red telephone box but what an amazing atmosphere once inside. The memory of playing there has really made me smile.

As Day 4 draws to a close, with a good few miles already under our belt, it's time to park and rest up for the night just up the hill from the gallery and looking down on the beach to our left. Tomorrow we head back west towards London but don't worry, we're not going near the place. I shall hug the Thames Estuary on my right until I find a way of getting over to the other side, from Kent to Essex. Sleep well. 4 down, 76 to go. Suddenly it feels a bit of a daunting task doesn't it?

Day 5

The journey on our 5th day, as we leave Margate on Canterbury Road, can hardly be called spectacular. The murky brown water of the grubby Thames isn't a pretty sight as it waves goodbye to England and heads out into The North Sea, leaving its prams and supermarket trolleys behind. When snow drops from the sky this particular part of England always seems to be hit the most with numerous road closures and accidents. My dear old mum loved the snow, she used to say it was the only time our garden looked as pretty as next door's.

On the opposite side of the road is an endless line of stationary European trucks waiting to get back home. Brexit has reduced their numbers, but they still sit there like families of elephants queuing for water with their young ones in tow. There seems to be a shortage of truck drivers since lockdown but every truck in the queue seems to have one so I'm not too sure what all the fuss is about. The A28 is far too busy for me and so I head off in a northerly direction towards Westgate on Sea and Minnis Bay.

So where will day 5 take us today? Somewhere beyond Southend I would imagine.

The A2 is such a boring road with very little to offer. There's Faversham where I played a folk club at The Chimney Boy and Gravesend, where I performed at The Woodville Theatre, a town so named because that's where the lines of graves of those who died from the plague ended, and that's about it. In the distance is The Queen Elizabeth 11 Bridge that spans the Thames across to Essex, known as The Dartford Crossing. It was named after a queen who obviously did nothing regarding the building of the thing so really it could have been inappropriately named after anyone I suppose. When travelling from south to north you travel under The Thames and not over it, through Dartford Tunnel. This is interesting. It first opened in 1963, 150 feet underwater and they decided to charge drivers to pass through until the bridge was paid for, not unlike William Pitt bringing in Income Tax to pay for a war. Wouldn't you think, after 60 years, the tunnel's construction has been paid for? It doesn't appear to be the case.

To cross The River Thames I almost need to join the dreaded M25 motorway, a circular lump of concrete that I absolutely hate, and pay the said fee for the awful experience, but it didn't happen, almost but not quite, thus keeping my journey's pledge that not a single mile of motorway would be used at any time on the entire trip around the whole of Britain. I definitely wasn't going to be beaten early doors by the horrendous M25.

It's a right turn away from London's Canary Wharf that we see in the distance. There used to be a Holiday Inn on the south side of the tunnel where I managed to get very drunk on many's the tour after shows at The Orchard Theatre in Dartford, but I can't seem to find it between the sprawl of container units and industrial eyesores that have sprung up since. There used to be a tree there somewhere, but I can't see that either. I seemed to upgrade my career in Dartford, just as I had in Brighton, from The Railway Hotel pub to the Mick Jagger Centre, before finally reaching the dizzy heights of sell-out concerts at The Orchard Theatre.

Over on the Essex side it's only a few miles before I turn right once more to head further away from London, towards the windy east coast. Although the road is new it's the site of The Circus Tavern, a nightclub that I played more times than I care to remember. It was East London's only nightclub and it was full of men wearing kipper ties and tables filled with the remains of chickens in baskets. First prize in the raffle may well have been a set of hubcaps or a new clutch for a Ford Cortina. I seem to remember being told you could buy house wine there by the slice, but I adored the character of the place and loved performing there. Before performing there myself I'd never set foot in a nightclub in my life. Nice memories indeed from my old stomping ground and don't forget that if there hadn't ever been any nightclubs the nation would have been overrun with chickens.

Goodbye Dartford and The Thames and hello Tilbury and The Thameside Theatre, Grays, on the north side.

Now the Thames Estuary is to our right as we hug the coast and make our way along the A13 to Southend, home of the longest pier in the world, a mile long as it tries to escape Essex and make its new home in Kent, nestled between the apple orchards and oasthouses.

Interestingly there are 56 piers sticking out from Britain's coastline, many for no real reason, just survivors of the Victorian era when people only paddled in the sea as opposed to went swimming like Matthew Webb. They didn't even strip off, it wasn't the done thing so the only way to be in the sea was to walk out on one of the 56. It's so strange to glance at old photographs that show dressed women paddling in the sea but holding umbrellas so they didn't get wet.

This particular pier is so long it had a green train taking you to the end and back again for no real reason as it was the same view as Kent as you could see from the shore. Oh well, people travelled on it anyway.

On my way to Southend it's a must to keep to the coast rive via Benfleet and drive the perimeter of Canvey Island, a place that, in 1953, realised it hadn't built its sea wall high enough. My Uncle Ted and Auntie Elsie lived in Ash Road and my first holidays were there, dog-sitting their pets, Tiny and Scamp, when Ted and Elsie went off on a more distant, far more exotic holiday of their own. It's only right and respectful to take one last look at the place where I listened to Radio Luxemburg for the first time on my brother's transistor radio.

Kings Nightclub on Canvey was my second nightclub gig after The Circus Tavern. I didn't quite know what to expect in those nightclubs and neither did the audience. Anyway, I negotiate Canvey Island and add 14 miles to add to my total mileage for my troubles.

Back on the mainland and through Leigh on Sea, a popular residential area for London's cab drivers, I finally reach Southend and The Cliffs Pavilion Theatre looking out to sea, theatre I played 14 times. Out the other side of town is The Roslyn Hotel in Thorpe Bay, one of my favourite overnights. I notice it's been re-named The Roslyn Beach Hotel and I'm curious to see how many tons of sand they must have dumped beside The Thames Estuary to call it that as I don't seem to recall much of a beach. I think it was here that I first realised how bloody noisy a seagull can be first thing in the morning. They always have something to moan about, like a miserable next-door neighbour. The friendlier you try to be the more they attack and the more chips they steal.

So many times I had my breakfast here at The Roslyn, looking out over the mudbanks of the estuary at absolutely nothing in particular before heading off to another venue on my tours with my stomach full of sausage, egg and bacon, not forgetting mushrooms, tinned tomatoes and baked beans. We used to call it a road crash because that is exactly what it looked like, a road crash on a plate. Suddenly, I was re-living it all again, this time being more careful with my diet. Yes, it was all coming back to me, like the fried bread often did on my previous visits. An ideal place to park up and take in the view and the memories one more time. Breakfast in the morning will be nothing more than a bowl of instant porridge and not a road-crash as I learnt my lesson years ago.

I used to love Southend, the kiss-me-quick hats and the candyfloss, until they built the country's VAT offices there and suddenly it wasn't quite as alluring as it used to be. It's funny how just one sinister building can take the shine off a place. It had a different atmosphere when we went to see the Christmas lights along the promenade. It wasn't exactly Blackpool but we had a game of our own, counting the number of lightbulbs that had blown. That must have been a hell of a job for one council-worker and his stepladder.

Similar to Southampton, Dartford and Brighton, there are so many music venues bouncing around in my head, places I played it after growing too old for the amusement arcades where I bunged endless pennies into a slot machine to try and win a single-finger Kit-Kat. From The Hoe club in Benfleet, The Railway Folk Club, to the heady heights of The Cliffs Pavilion and Princes Theatre in the town. Ah yes, Southend, the southern end of Essex, has so many good times to recall and I recall them all today before tipping my baseball cap to a place that had so much importance for me in so many different ways.

Day 6

There used to be lots of little towns and villages to the east of Southend, places like Westcliff and Shoeburyness, but they have all joined together over the years and now are all possibly considered to be part of Southend. It's tempting to head directly north towards Chelmsford from here, but that would defeat the coastline plan and so we keep to the east as we explore Great Wakering and Foulness Island, a popular bird sanctuary, popular for birds anyway. I soon realise that birds that amass there don't need roads and so I head back west for 3 miles before heading north once again.

Eventually we reach Burnham on Crouch, an upmarket area where posh Essex people moor their posh weekend boats and wear posh quilted waistcoats and posh dark blue deck-shoes. It's a beautiful spot, posh but beautiful and a nice place to stop for lunch for some, but not me as I'm skipping lunch to head on down the creek to Battlesbridge where King Canute tried to turn the tide with the wave of his hand to no avail, the silly man. The estuary is tidal here and so most of the boats are lop-sided, as if they'd had too much to drink at The Circus Tavern the night before.

Battlesbridge, where I use my mass intelligence to work out a battle once took place here on a bridge, has a large gathering of antique shops by the mill adjacent to the old bridge, empty on weekdays and rammed solid with people at weekends, and here we find a wonderful, old-fashioned eating house where I can take my foot off the clutch for a while and fill my stomach with a decent meal. I don't remember the last time I drank tea from a cup and saucer, but today's the day.

I once played the village hall here for my Auntie May who was raising money for Meals On Wheels. She's long gone now but I think fondly of her as I eat my dinner, remembering how I spent every Christmas at her house when I was a kid. Ah yes, the good old selection box, every kid had one, containing Fry's Chocolate Creams, Caramac which was a weird beige coloured chocolate, Tiffin and an out of place tube of fruit gums, so named because they stuck to your gums for hours. Everyone had a selection box at some time in their lives and they were far more fun than Easter Eggs. Are you, like me, old enough to remember when they used to put chocolates inside Easter Eggs and didn't cheat by not bothering because it became a darn sight easier to just increase the packaging and put stuff like chocolate bars next to the egg? What happened to the excitement of smashing an Easter Egg to pieces to see what was inside? Young people today just haven't lived. Smashing Easter Eggs and hitting Brazil nut toffee with a hammer was all part of becoming a bit of a James Dean rebel back in the day. In the East End of London it was our first taste of hooliganism.

The 6th day of the coastal journey around Britain is now complete, not too spectacular scenery-wise during the morning, as I mentioned earlier, but it brought back lots of wonderful distant memories. Tomorrow, still resisting the inland diversion to Chelmsford, where Marconi began his radio career, we will be heading northward along the coast to one of my favourite English counties, Suffolk, that's once we have finished negotiating what's left of North Essex and The River Crouch that's been somewhat in the way, thus the cause of such an enforced diversion. Suffolk obviously refers to folk who lived in the south and Norfolk is much the same for folk who lived further north, so I can't help wondering why Essex wasn't called Eastfolk. It would have made sense and it would have also added to cockney rhyming slang too. North and south, mouth, east and west, chest. It's incredible what mindless nonsense runs through your brain when you are sitting behind a steering-wheel for hours on end. I'll check the oil in the VW too, it seems to have developed a kind of smoker's cough. Goodnight fellow travellers.

Day 7

One week in and all going well. Up bright and early with the wind in our sails as we head exactly due north for the first time on our journey. Today, with a modicum of luck, I will make it through no less than three different counties, Essex, Suffolk and Norfolk, with so many more personal memories in abundance. The plan is to make it up to Cromer, in North Norfolk where the crabs live, by close of play tomorrow night, so it's a two-day assault on this particular part of Britain.

Still in Essex, with The North Sea raging to our right, it's off to the seaside resort of Clacton. Well, it used to be when I was a kid, but now I realise it's more a home for the elderly, often nicknamed God's waiting room for obvious reasons. Jokes about Clacton are plentiful. For example, it's a great place for comedy because the audience are pissing themselves before the show starts. The shop windows are bi-focal, a constant rainbow overhead and so on. Yet there is something quaint about Clacton and its wrought iron balconies. Even the enchanting Westcliff Theatre resembles an oversized army hut but a much friendlier venue than The Princes Theatre down the road. It really is Old England for Old English people, and probably a few Old English Sheepdogs too I wouldn't doubt.

I never came here as a kid but spent various fortnights at neighbouring St Osyth and Jaywick Sands. Our rented caravan in Jaywick was named Leswick and it was about the size of a canteen teapot. It didn't matter, we were beside the sea and that's all that mattered, just like today's drive. I would love to drop in on those places for a second glance, but they aren't on my agenda this time, what with the miles that lay ahead and the strict route I have planned.

We cross the unarmed, unmanned border into Suffolk. I love this area of Essex and Suffolk so much because it's John Constable country. Unfortunately, we can't visit Flatford Mill and stare at Willy Lott's cottage that he painted in his Haywain picture as, like Chelmsford, it's too far inland, so we head for the equally inspiring town of Southwold in East Suffolk. This place is decadent in the extreme.

The River Blyth heads inland here from the sea and originally, according to The Domesday Book, it was a fishing port long before it became a town that proudly boasts that half its population comprises of wealthy second-home dwellers. To buy a nice house in Southwold may take a lottery win for most of us, such is the beauty and appeal of the place, all of which comes at quite a hefty price. Strangely, there is no mention of The Lottery in The Domesday Book.

In all my years on the road I never played Southwold, or The Maltings nearby, although I performed at the nearby Riverside Theatre in Woodbridge many times. It was, and probably still is, all a bit posh for my crowd and so, just like today, I would usually travel 11 miles of the A12, up the coast to perform in good old Lowestoft. Before I could afford the room rates of The Imperial Hotel I used to stay in a bed and breakfast here that was so drab they used to tie a teabag to the hot-water bottle.

It's so sad that Lowestoft has seen better times, before a vibrant herring fishing industry fell into deep decline, taking the town with it. Sometimes it's easy to forget we live on an island surrounded by fish with fleets of trawlers once heading off from all quarters of our nation. No wonder we invented the fish and chip shop and the pickled onion factory. I played The Marina Theatre here many times, before I opted to play The Seagull Theatre instead, and I still recall its bright green seats so it would appear I didn't sell it out too often or I would never have seen the colour of the seats. Then there is Hopton Holiday Village right on the coast, now home of The Bowls Championships on TV, a venue that booked me with great regularity as the owners were fellow West Ham supporters. Lowestoft never quite hit the dizzy seaside heights of Great Yarmouth, just 10 miles further north, and I still don't know why as I sit and reflect.

The beaches along this coastline are so savagely underrated as there are miles of beautiful sands all along this side of Britain. It's a bit on the windy side though so not too popular with men who wear wigs or have loose-fitting false teeth that would chatter away with the cold until they fell out. Do men still wear wigs? If so, we should take our hats off to them, once the wind has died down of course.

So Lowestoft has taken a battering in more ways than one and yet it's one of Britain's first ever settlements. Years ago they found flint tools here that date back 700,000 years. They found such tools in The East End of London too but they came to the conclusion they had probably been stolen. I'm not too sure of the derivation of Lowes, but toft was an old Scandinavian word for homestead and that's all I know. They all sailed over here, ranting and bellowing, and took over the place, thousands of men in longboats who all looked like the two male members of Abba.

Nowadays, looking out at The North Sea from Lowestoft it now seems to be nothing more than a giant carpark for oilrigs and wind turbines. I lose count as I scan the horizon. Wind turbines fascinate me. Just like seagulls, they're ok at a distance but when you get up close they're huge, white menacing-looking things. We all think they're the new green source of energy but they're not actually that new when you think about it. Take a look at a wind turbine and you will discover it's nothing more than a skinny, white windmill, and they've been around for hundreds of years as a source of energy. Yes, upon closer observation they are nothing more than great big versions of those whirly things we used to stick in the tops of sandcastles when we were kids.

Day 8

You may well know there is another Yarmouth on The Isle of Wight that doesn't call itself great. In fact, it doesn't even call itself average. It's just plain and simple Yarmouth and the place leaves you to decide for yourself if it's great or not. The naming of the Norfolk version goes back to the 13th Century when it was called Great Yarmouth so as not to be confused with Little Yarmouth that sits on the other side of The River Yare. Locals still insist on calling the place Great Yarmouth and none of us seem to have a problem with that so let's just take their word for it and take a quick drive around. Hang on a moment, there's a folksong titled Shoals of Herring and there's no mention of Great when Yarmouth is included in the first verse. Now we're all confused.

Great Yarmouth is a mass of holiday parks, caravan sites and bed and breakfast establishments a-plenty. They don't compare with big daddy Skegness further north, as we shall discover later no doubt, but there's lots of them just the same. My first summer season was here when the place boasted three vibrant theatres, The Wellington Pier, The Britannia Pier and the ABC Theatre further into the town. Adjacent to The Britannia, where I performed for 12 weeks, was The George Hotel that had a wonderful cellar bar that never seemed to close. All the acts from all three theatres mustered there after shows and spent hours recalling showbiz stories of old until it got light next morning. I treated my daughter Polly to her first visit to the circus here in Great Yarmouth too, courtesy of owner Peter Jay, and she laughed her head off as monkeys rode pigs around the circus ring. Ha, those were the days, that sort of thing used to be allowed back then. Is it allowed these days? Monkey jockeys? I have no idea, but it all came back to me as we continued north to my final destination of the day, Cromer, waving goodbye to many great times both Great Yarmouth and Lowestoft had spared me during my long life on the road. Onwards and northwards.

By the way, did you know that jockeys aren't allowed to grow beards due to some stupid ancient ruling? Well, monkeys are covered in the stuff and so I doubt if it's allowed anymore after all, politically correct or not.

Well, I've made it to Cromer and I will enjoy a day here tomorrow. I think the camper van needs a rest more than me.

Day 9

Another town and another pier to feast my eyes upon. I still play the Cromer Folk Festival every year and I know the town well, particularly what claims to be the best fish and chip shop in the country on the sea front. Haddock and chips are its speciality and it's there we will have our dinner this evening, looking out towards the lifeboat station, me knowing many of the Davies family associated with it, before getting our heads down for the night in the car park opposite. None of this Welcome Break motorway services bollocks where they fine you £100 for staying more than two hours if you're having a meal and a quick snooze before you continue on your journey. I hate those money-grabbing places so much that I'd rather run out of petrol than give them my hard-earnt cash, though I must admit I use their toilets from time to time, quite often actually, my way of leaving a deposit. I suppose you could say it's a place where I just go through the motions. I wasn't to collide with any such harsh places throughout my 6,000-mile journey, I made sure of that, a decision helped by avoiding motorways at all costs.

Cromer is far more civilised than those rip-off services areas cropping up with alarming regularity on our big arterial roads, so is a disorderly Wembley football crowd to be fair. This town is far kinder and more understanding and a great place to end the day before working our way along the hump at the top of Norfolk towards Hunstanton and beyond. Tomorrow will be a beautiful chilled-out drive and the wind will drop as the coastline turns west. No wonder crabs walk sideways. They need to keep out of the wind too. This is where the men probably put their wigs back on with some kind of relief.

Cromer is over 250 miles distant from our starting point of Southampton as the crow flies or as the crab walks sideways, but I've driven considerably more. It's a small percentage of our journey completed with a good few thousand miles still to go. The VW camper van is now well stocked with an array of glucose sweets and energy drinks, but still not a Satnav in sight. No miles under my belt today but that's fine as it's all part of my grand scheme, covering as many miles as I can when I have the energy and then calming down from time to time as I progress, making the most of places very special to me. How can such a small island be so full of interest? I've already name-checked 25 theatres where I performed at some point in my career, already accounting for over 150 shows, and we've barely started. I may well need to adjust my predictions.

Cromer is a town where time, thankfully, stood still. The Pavilion Theatre, home of the folk festival, Folk On The Pier, was hit by a massive storm in 2013 and when I performed there that year the audience had to walk around a huge hole that appeared in the wooden flooring of the pier that year, by the box office, but in true theatrical tradition, the show went on. Of all the theatres in the land it's one of my favourites when considering the tedious periods between soundcheck and show, normally between 6pm and 8pm, because I love to nip out of the stage door at the back, at the end of the pier by the lifeboat station and watch the old boys bass fishing. They're wonderful old boys, all with a fisherman's story to tell.

The only major problem with The Pavilion Theatre is there is no parking facility, not even on the road at the entrance to the pier and it's a hell of a walk from the carpark carrying equipment down a massive slope and along the pier to the stage. Returning after a show is always an even more daunting climb, but today is different, no show and no equipment to carry.

I'm really chilled as it's all a far cry from the hustle and bustle of the crossing of The River Thames and the hectic driving through Southend and even Canvey Island. This is far more peaceful and more the kind of thing I looked forward to when I planned the journey some months ago. It's strange when you plan such a lengthy project as this you can't help thinking the entire coastline is all country lanes and tranquillity when it actually isn't at times. Having said that, we've reached a delightful area of tranquillity today. Just what I looked forward to.

Day 10

Good morning. It's a beautiful morning and we're setting off nice and early before we collide with hectic commuters heading for Norwich who don't want to be stuck behind a VW camper van on their way to work. There's a good few miles to negotiate westward before we head north once again. This top part of Norfolk, its hump if you like, is beautiful and beneath us are The Norfolk Broads, a part of the country I visited every year with children and friends and it's the home of The Maddermarket Theatre, Norwich, where I hosted one of my first art exhibitions. I loved hiring a boat and travelling around at 4mph spotting herons and finding pubs like The Swan at Horning and another beauty at Salthouse whose name I can't recall. Yes, it's all below us now as we hug the coastline once again. This area is popular with celebrities who want to live quiet lives away from stage and screen. I know a few of them but it would be completely remiss of me to name them and ruin their privacy.

Ah, Overstrand, Sheringham, Wells on Sea, truly unspoilt countryside and a few neglected roads above the A149 that test the springs of the VW. All motorists drive much slower in sedate Norfolk than on any other part of the journey so far and we even manage to overtake a woman in a clapped-out Ford Fiesta. Now there's a result for the VW. I have a funny feeling she must have nodded off because most of the time my poor old VW couldn't even overtake a granny pushing her grandchildren in a pram, let alone someone in a car no matter how old the vehicle and the driver happens to be.

41

The Royal Estate of Sandringham. The place where Royals spend their Christmases, sits just to the right and down a bit of the coastal town of Hunstanton and the town's Princess Theatre, ironic in the extreme, is where Princess Diana used to take her young children, William and Harry, to watch the local pantomime. It all seems so long ago when we consider the trials and tribulations that have befallen the three of them in different ways.

This part of Norfolk smells of lavender and I think more is grown here than anywhere else in the country. Honestly, it's like walking into a bathroom when you've just run the bath water rather than driving along a road.

I must have played the Hunstanton theatre a dozen times or more and I always loved the spare time between soundcheck and showtime here too, the same as Cromer, during which I always visited the world's biggest joke shop on the other side of the road to the stage door. I've often wondered how they knew they were the biggest joke shop in the whole world as it's quite a boast.

Every year, when playing The Princess Theatre, I did most of my Christmas shopping here which thus explains the odd and desperately unwanted presents I used to buy for my family and friends. I think they were all pleased when I stopped performing at The Princess Theatre a few years ago and presented them with nicer presents, far more appealing than fart powder, exploding cigarettes and plastic Elvis Presley wigs. Mind you, I always wrapped them all nicely, the presents I'm talking about and not the family and friends. Isn't it the thought that counts? If you had asked my family and friends a few years ago the answer would have been a definitive no. It all made me wonder if the Royals have the same idea for Christmas morning. No wonder they all seem to argue so much.

A nice place to stay, mingled in with the sand dunes by Le Strange Hotel. Glancing across the sea to my right I espy the next piece of Britain I shall be visiting tomorrow. I need to drop south in the morning to get me round a vast estuary.

Day 11

Eleven days on the road and we haven't done too bad considering we're in a vintage vehicle with a vintage driver taking all the longest routes from town to town. So where are we heading? Hopefully we will spend night 11 in Grimsby, ambitious but we'll give it a go. Obviously if we were travelling as the crow flies we would be further up north by the end of the day but this is an unfair part of the coastal drive with all its ins and outs, westward and then eastward, so reaching Grimsby will be a serious result if we make it. Do crows always fly straight anyway I ask myself.

Travelling westward beyond the rim of Norfolk we could easily find ourselves in Peterborough or Cambridge if we veered off the coast road. It really is quite deceptive that we're now way up into The Midlands and even beyond, when it all seems nothing more than an extension of a trip through Essex and the lower situated counties of England from a few days ago. It's so deceptive.

Leaving the Norfolk hump behind we touch the very edge of East Cambridgeshire before sweeping round in a giant curve and our tyres hit the roads of Lincolnshire and we head directly northwards again. Dead straight roads all the way for a while, that's Lincolnshire for you. It's interesting to think that by the time we reach the tip of this county, probably before the end of tomorrow night, we would have by-passed Rutland, Leicestershire, Nottinghamshire, Derbyshire and even South Yorkshire, all land-locked counties that do not reach as high up the map as the tip of Lincolnshire. It's amazing as Lincolnshire doesn't seem that big or important at first glance, what with not having a top cricket team or any top-level football club to boast of, but there's more to a county than that. Some would say it has very little apart from the legend of Robin Hood, an odd chap who hung out in a forest with men wearing green tights, if he ever lived anywhere at all, and the pungent smell from endless cabbage fields replacing the lavender of Norfolk, but that would be so far from the truth as we will discover as we make our way up the county. For instance, there's The Theatre Royal in Lincoln where author Jeffrey Archer worked as a stagehand whilst serving his prison sentence for some crime or other that has never really interested me. I always stayed at The Post Office, next to Lincoln Cathedral, well knowing its bells would give me an early morning call, but not tonight thank you. Lincoln Cathedral was the tallest building in Britain for 250 years from the 13th Century, until its spire collapsed and then I assume it was one of the shortest. Another interesting fact about this place is that The Romans built The Fossdyke Navigation Canal 2,000 years ago and it's the oldest canal in Britain that's still in use today. It's a kind of Roman landmark of achievement as the can is where the famous Fosse Way, the 200-mile road from Exeter to Lincoln, comes to an end. Just imagine the ecstasy of completing such long road only to be told it was time to start digging out trenches in preparation for the canal's construction. That must have knocked the stuffing out of them.

Along the southern coast of Lincolnshire the area of Norfolk we passed through yesterday is seen across The Wash, the drains in the fields are plentiful and not a lot else until we espy the thousands, possibly millions, of gleaming white caravans engulfing Skegness, looking as if they're gathering like an army about to attack Scandinavia from the west.

The Great British Folk Festival, where I've appeared on two occasions, takes place at Butlins every year in Skeggy. It's a very rare indoor festival and they even supply chalets for the performers, a free luxury in my musical world. Few would ever think of bringing together Butlins Holiday Camp and a folk festival in the same breath, but it really works, apart from the fact it takes place the first week in December and it's always freezing cold. I always think of a festival as a gathering in a field, enjoying the sun and a few beers, but The Great British Folk Festival breaks that image with great success.

Dotted around the area are a multitude of freshwater fishing lakes that I often visit to partake in my favourite pastime when I have time off, but no time for that on this trip, plus the fact I'd have to deviate inland to reach freshwater stretches of rivers and lakes, far away from where I'm heading today.

I did say Grimsby was a hell of a plan and I have to report that I never quite made it, but it doesn't matter. It's a long straight road out of Skegness with numerous lay-bys and parking areas so let's call it a day.

Blimey, I didn't know there were this many white caravans in the whole world, let alone in Skegness. It definitely isn't the place to walk to the pub and partake in excess alcohol because you'd never find your caravan amongst the multitudes when the pub closes and you walk back in the dark. I think if I owned one here I'd have to paint mine luminous orange so I stood a reasonable chance of finding it again in a drunken state. I wonder if posties have to deliver letters to such caravans. I have no idea but I don't think it's a job I'd want to take on.

Skegness is a strange, worshipped and spoken so highly of by Those who live in the north of England, yet most of the population of Britain, especially southerners and the Welsh, barely know of the place, let alone stay there for a couple of weeks on holiday. It may well be considered as the last bastion of the north and south divide. If you're not sure I suggest you walk into a fish and chip shop and see what's on the menu, as I have just done. Having said all of that it's a place that holds nice memories for me and it's been a pleasure to visit here on my special journey.

Day 12

We awake early, as we do each morning, and after a quick splash and scrubbing of teeth we edge on to Chapel St Leonards, through Mablethorpe and then onwards until we finally reach Grimsby, albeit rather late. This part of the journey barely needs a steering wheel as it's such a long, straight part of our trip, just like yesterday, a chance to take things easy before the sharp bends and climbs awaiting us up in Scotland in the not-too-distant future. That's the compelling thing about Britain, it's so very different every way you turn a corner or drive a few miles. Most countries cannot boast such variation in such a vast quantity. Lincolnshire is at an end soon and we will experience a different coastline with greater gradients.

It was Gerry Rafferty who wrote the song lyrics 'clowns to the left of me jokers to the right,' but if he were with us today it would be 'cabbages to the left of me North Sea to the right.' No wonder the smell of Lincolnshire always reminds me of school dinners. Oh yes, good old school dinners, finding a shiny spoon and licking it so nobody stole it casserole with skin on top so it can be sliced into eight and wondering about the flavour of pink custard. I digress.

Not so long-ago Grimsby boasted the world's largest fishing fleet, second to none many said, but the famous Cod War changed all that, followed, as if that wasn't bad enough, by Brexit regulations. Ah yes, The Cod War, an easy skirmish against Iceland when compared to the two World Wars we'd fought against Germany in the 20th Century and yet the outcome was equally as devastating to Grimsby's main industry at the time.

The Scandinavian Danes settled here in the 9th Century and a grim is the word for a Danish fisherman in their own language. By is the old Norse word for small village and so they put the two words together and, bingo, Grimsby came to be, as simple as that. It has artistic connections with Bernie Taupin, Elton John's lyricist, coming from and having written about Grimsby. Then of course there is Rod Temperton, the songwriter who wrote Michael Jackson's Thriller. Oh yes, Grimsby has much to boast about in the musical world.

The Grimsby Auditorium, where I performed in 2004, is a majestic theatre and it's a spectacular and, dare I say, unexpected piece of architecture, nothing quite what you would expect, but, having marvelled at the place, I must head north once again as I eventually choose to park up for the night under the lengthy shadows of The Humber Bridge beside yet another venue, The Ropewalk Theatre at Barton Upon Humber. It's an unspoilt building of historic interest, an unbelievably long building where long lengths of rope were entwined. The theatre itself is at the front and the parking area gives views of old and modern caught between the old factory and the new bridge.

It would have been 238 miles from Southampton to Grimsby on a standard drive, but it has been considerably more as I kept to the coast. I have a funny feeling I've doubled that distance taking my chosen route. Oh yes, I must be approaching 500 miles by now. Tonight I'm weary and I can but only imagine how The Proclaimers must have felt after they walked a bit further than this. Yes, walked, they didn't have a faithful VW camper van to ease their burden. No comfy seats and a small cooker on board, no sneaky afternoon nap in a lay-by. Those two lads are too cool for their own good and I'll tell them so when I turn right at Edinburgh and make my way to Fife, their part of Scotland. Here's a thought, if you were walking 500 miles to see your girlfriend would you take your brother with you? Exactly. Just imagine walking that far only to find the girl has gone shopping and isn't home.

In the meantime, it's time to sleep off that long, straight road and celebrate the fact I didn't nod off whilst behind the wheel.

Day 13

When I became a musician, a travelling troubadour all those years ago, there was no such thing as The Humber Bridge as it was still on the drawing board. Apparently they'd spoken about it for 50 years but they never pressed the green light. It's quite comforting to know that councils, councillors and their senses of urgency haven't changed through the years. I'd already been on the road for 15 years when it opened in 1981. That last sentence made me smile. Do bridges actually open? I know shops, cans and mouths open, but can you actually open a bridge or just make it available to use? Yet another stupid thought as I drive, I grant you.

People either side of The Humber, a wide river in the extreme, rarely met, let alone spoke to each other unless they risked a somewhat hazardous ferry journey. From Barton, where I slept last night, across to Hessle on the other side, it's a walk of 1.4 miles, making it the longest bridge to walk across in the whole world. The bridge reduced travel time from Grimsby to Hull in Humberside by half, from 82 miles to 41. So over we go and don't look down.

Hull ahead and musical Grimsby behind me now have so much in common. To those who live far from both of them they are still thought of as large fishing ports, but time has moved on since those days of brave men taking on The North Sea to put food on the table. Yes, it still happens but not at the same level as before. Hull became a cultural centre of Britain and its marina is as classy as Chelsea or Brighton. Hull City Hall is a splendid, masonic-looking building that I first played with folk band Steeleye Span and its stone interior is as grand as its outside. Although we mention Span in the same part of the book as The Humber Bridge, there is no connection. The name of the band comes from a traditional folksong in which John 'Steeleye' Span had a fist fight with John Bowlin and the band name was suggested by Martin Carthy, our greatest traditional singer and resident of this part of Britain. A slight diversion there but worthy of a mention.

From Hull the coast seems to lean to the left, as if the whole island is leaning forward putting its boots on or whispering to Ireland. Humberside as a county no longer exists as it was abolished in 1996, but it was Humberside when I began singing in folk clubs and so, in my head, Humberside still remains. Anyway, it's tiny compared to other counties so there's no need to bully it and deny it an existence.

As I drive along I realise, for some strange reason that's beyond me, there are no big football clubs at all on this side of the country until we go further north towards Newcastle. No Premier League clubs in Kent, Essex, Suffolk or Lincolnshire. How odd. Pointless, boring observation but a fact just the same. They probably found better things to do over this side of the country than watch a bunch of overpaid kids trip over ants and break their legs. To labour the point further, Grimsby Football Club don't even play in Grimsby, so theoretically they never have home games. Yes, ok, I take the point and you're right. It all changes anyway when the camper van reaches the north-east, but until then there is little or no top football clubs, or heavy industry for that matter, on the east coast of England, possibly with the exception of the steel industry that has suffered in the same way as the fishing industry in recent times.

This journey I'm undertaking around Britain makes me realise how different this island is in terms of the way people live and have lived depending on where they lived, if that makes sense. The reassurance is they have the common factor of all having local theatres that have stayed open for many years. By all accounts there are over 1,000 theatres in Britain and probably the same number of cinemas that used to be theatres before they went through their biological changes.

Day 14

Two weeks ago today we began our journey and I'm beginning to sense that Scotland is only a few days away now as, by the end of today, I would have almost been all the way up the east side of England. I reckon another 2 days will do the trick. I'm excited.

There's only 37 miles between Hull and Scarborough which we shall now negotiate and with luck we will reach Newcastle by nightfall and put paid to the lack of those big football clubs on our journey, not that we give a toss, just an observation as I mentioned before.

There are 48 counties in England alone and today we smash our way through 4 of them in one foul swoop, a hell of an achievement in an ancient VW camper van. Whilst doing so we stop off at Scarborough Castle where I spent the night under the stars on my way to college in Glasgow in the 1960s, the first and last time I'd ever done such a thing as there were too many scuffling noises and creepy things for my liking. I've never been one for camping, even getting my mum to write a sicknote when I joined the cubs and they set up a camping weekend in Epping Forest. It's so strange that camping has never interested me and yet I love living in the camper van for a few months so much that words fail me, not a great thing when you're trying to write a book.

Britain's coastline really is at its best here. 15 miles north of Scarborough, in North Yorkshire, is Robin Hood's Bay, a place that actually exists unlike its namesake, and then a further 6 miles along an enchanting coastline and passing through Sneaton, is Whitby. They have a folk festival here and it's one that, in its wisdom some would say, has never booked me so I have no story to relate I'm afraid. It's stunning though, even if the VW isn't too keen on the steep gradients. Suffolk and Norfolk it isn't and Lincolnshire it definitely isn't.

Greenery becomes sparser, making way for far more houses the further north I drive until we eventually reach our base for tonight, Newcastle, a strange name as there is no such thing as a new castle, just look at the lack of roofs and windows, their builders never finished a single one. It takes many miles of built-up area to get anywhere near Newcastle city centre, but it's here somewhere, through this sprawl of townhouses and main roads I need to avoid to stay close to the east coast.

Arriving In Newcastle allows me to boast the fact, through these pages, that I ran The Great North Run twice alongside my mate Carol Vorderman. My lungs shudder as I even think about it now. On the first occasion I recall The Red Arrows nearly knocked my head off as they went over and I wasn't happy because they were cheating. Anyone can do The Great North Run in a plane, so they were just showing off in my humble opinion. It was only a couple of miles from the start, admittedly uphill, to the Tyne Bridge when I realised I'd made a huge mistake. Yes, 2 miles and I was totally knackered by the time I got there. In fact, I was so exhausted I had to stop and have a cigarette.

Despite such tiring memories I really do now sense Scotland in the distance, once Northumberland has been negotiated tomorrow. The straight distance from Southampton to Newcastle is 322 miles, double that distance for me as I have mentioned so many times before, so I feel well and truly into my journey around the coastline of Britain. I wouldn't be at all surprised if I haven't driven 1,000 miles. It's difficult to work out mileage while I've been backwards and forwards on the smaller roads. So many of those baby ones have taken me into a small town or village and then back out again before I drove into the sea, so I don't really have much idea.

Tonight we pitch up at Gosforth Park, north of Newcastle, before continuing on for 63 miles to Berwick Upon Tweed and then into Bonnie Scotland where my folk music career began as a student. I can't wait. But first, the giant hurdle that is still Newcastle, much as I'm trying to distract myself. Not knowing the area too well, I was hoping to cross The Tyne Bridge in all its splendour and history, just like I did in shorts and trainers, but it never happened. I must have gone through some tunnel or other as I'm now the other side of the mighty river.

There are so many traditional folksongs that mention The Tyne as well as more modern-day songs. It's probably second only to London. I love the fact that The Bridge Folk Club, the second oldest club in Britain, help the students studying The Newcastle University Folk and Traditional Music Course. It's only right when you remember much of the folk scene in the 1960s was built in colleges and universities, including my own in Glasgow.

Newcastle brought back so many memories as I drove through, my regular appearances on Tyne Tees Television on the Late Show with Gillian Reynolds, taking my BBC Radio 2 show there with Andy Alyffe and the various folk clubs I played there over the years. It's a big old place, that's for sure, but I wanted to drive through as quickly as I could and return to the coastline that I'd been forced away from to get through the big city. How many times did I play Newcastle City Hall? I've no idea. I never headlined there, not one of my stronger areas, but I supported Jethro Tull, Steeleye Span, Joan Armatrading and Tom Jones, so I played there a few times for sure. I did headline at The Customs House Theatre in South Shields though, a splendid venue with an adjacent fish and chip shop worthy of note, right up there with the Cromer equivalent.

I may be wrong, and I probably am, but I'm about to travel on what I think may be the only major arterial road that runs along any part of the British coastline, the A1. Can this really be true? Surely not. At Gosforth Park I can travel east and re-join the A1 further up country so I don't miss out on any of this stunning north-eastern coast. It's rugged and fits in with the hard lives the locals here experienced throughout history, working underground or out at sea, even under the sea. I look forward to travelling along this part of England tomorrow, beside mile after mile of dry-stone walls. Now those guys really were master builders who never had to wait for cement to dry.

To be honest I have no idea how long it took me to negotiate the width and length of Newcastle and its surrounding areas as it all became a bit of a blur of built-up roads and cranes reaching skyward. Suffice to say it was a good few hours and my brain is confused for the first time on the journey. I remember running through Gateshead on that Great North Run and some of the road-signs were vaguely familiar but I still wasn't sure where I was going, yet I somehow got through and out the other side of both this trip and the marathon. Of course the marathon was easier because I simply followed the bloke in front. This was different. I had a fear this would happen in Newcastle, Edinburgh and Glasgow, possibly a few more such as Liverpool and Blackpool. We shall see, although I have a hunch it will be three out of three. My navigational skills let me down big-time today but it doesn't matter and it will mean even less tomorrow. I have no time deadline and nowhere to be at any particular time, so I just shrug my shoulders at the occasional heavy traffic.

Day 15

Good morning Northumberland. Northumberland or Northumbria? I'm not too sure but we're here anyway. It's definitely colder up here than back home in Salisbury, so much so the van heater is on for the first time this trip. I use the term heater loosely, it wouldn't have helped Scott of The Antarctic's frostbite, that's for sure. It's the northern-most county of England and don't I know it. Black coffee boiled up on the stove and then away we go.

I only played The Alnwick Playhouse Theatre the once, oh and The Berwick on Tweed Maltings just the once too, so I'm very much the tourist today, the same as yourself. That doesn't mean I don't know much about this area or have any fond memories because I most certainly do and it's good to be back here to re-live some golden musical moments in my life, musical moments that would actually change my life, so a return was long overdue.

Nothing obstructs the beautiful coastal views as we head north, driving so close to the sea you feel you could almost get out and have a paddle or go crabbing for a couple of hours. The sea is blue and although it's still The North Sea by name it doesn't look anywhere near as forbidding as the same mass of water alongside Essex, Suffolk and Norfolk. It seems to be calmer, more tranquil, as if it's relaxing more as it has come north with us.

A gentle saunter takes us to the tiny fishing village of Seahouses, a major part of my musical upbringing, for it was here I sat on the harbour wall as a teenager and listened to some friends I met on holiday singing folk songs. I couldn't join in, I had few musical skills at the time, but I was mesmerised, so much so it played a major part in me leaving The Beatles and Rolling Stones behind as I discovered a new form of music, although I didn't realise it at the time, thus why I had to wait until my college days to make the full transition.

This place has changed beyond recognition since I was last here over half a century ago, hardly surprising of course, as I have to. There are far more houses and it's all more commercial now, but my memory takes me back to the seals, weaving in and out of the tiny fishing boats in the harbour and The Schooner pub, I think that's what it was called, come to think of it, it probably wasn't, at the end of Taylor Street where I bought my packets of Embassy tipped. I discovered folk music in all its glory when a student in Glasgow as you now know, but, yes, my first taste of the music I fell in love with was here, sitting on this harbour wall in Seahouses. I never met up with those singers again, never had a chance to thank them for the inspiration, but they are with us in spirit today, so thank you Margaret, Tommy and Tommy's sister. The town has doubled in size since I was last here over half a century ago and it doesn't seem so easy now just to saunter down to the harbour and sing a few songs without being bothered by others. Oh yes and another fish and chip springs to mind by the name of Mole's.

It's time to move on, time and tide wait for no man, and before long I stop the van to take in the rugged beauty of the Farne Islands and Lindisfarne on the top like a stone cherry. Wow. There were so many invasions went on here, thus so many ruined castles, as intruders tried to claim new territory a long way from their homes. Maybe I'm an intruder myself who's a long way from home, just like those who came across

60

The North Sea all those centuries ago. Bamburgh Castle, or what's left of it, looms in the distance, a tall monument of conflict past and then it's full throttle onwards to finally reach Berwick on Tweed. I'm just over 2 miles south of the Scottish border, Berwick is very much in England, even though its football team plays in the Scottish League to cut down on travelling and the subsequent costs. Oh no, more football club links. Berwick is the northernmost town in England and its actually further north than Copenhagen, the capital of Denmark.

Right now I'm more or less equidistant between Newcastle and Edinburgh and so the decision is made to change plan and make it to Scotland before nightfall. With the ragged rocks beneath us as I drive across the bridge over The Tweed, I arrive in Scotland. It makes me smile to see the petrol garage and services on the right-hand side of the road at a roundabout with a signpost that says fuel to the right and Scotland to the left. We take the left turn, cheering as we pass the sign that welcomes us into Scotland and we pull in at a lay-by that is surrounded by scrubland and heather. Oh yes, we're in Scotland alright. We turn around and drive back to the services in England, take on supplies, and dine on a wonderful fresh mackerel salad in the back of the VW.

It's this very evening that I realised why I wanted to make this trip in the first place, a journey around the perimeter of an island I thought I knew so well after 50 years of driving to and from its various far-flung outposts. Yes, I thought I knew it well but this evening I own up and admit I didn't know that much after all. Driving to theatres all my life is all very well but I now realise how seldom I took the time to absorb the various places of interest on offer. Scenic and industrial, ragged and built-up, it is all part of Britain, the place where I was born. That's the things about being on tour, you arrive in time for a soundcheck and then you're in a theatre until you leave for him in the darkness, ignoring everything else. I always knew I had to take this on one day and I'm so glad I have as it's a million miles from lockdown, this is true freedom of the road and I wouldn't have missed it for the world. Another thing, it wouldn't have been the same in a modern vehicle as VW offered a hippie slant that is all part of my memory bank. It has allowed me to drive at a slow pace and take it all in without annoying my fellow motorists.

It's time to celebrate the fact that I have successfully driven the entire length of England, all the way up the right-hand coastline and, as promised, I never used a motorway once, something I'm quite proud of, not even across The Thames from Dartford to Tilbury as I went underground and not over the bridge if you remember. How long ago does that couple of miles under The Thames seem now? Blimey, it seems like a previous life as I sit this far up north.

The usual mileage check, the more tedious as it's becoming by the day, driving directly from Southampton to Berwick Upon Tweed is 400 miles, but, once again to the point of boredom, that's using all the major roads, which we most certainly didn't. Checking my own mile gauge I do happen to know I have reached the 20% point of my journey around Britain. It seems a hell of a lot longer, especially as I have done the length of one side of the country, but 20% it is, nothing more than the commission fees of a crap agent who thinks he's worth more than what he thinks he's worth.

60 miles in the morning will find us on the outskirts of one of Britain's most beautiful cities, Edinburgh. Now we really are talking even more memories. A diversion first thing to visit Eyemouth and St Abbs before 25 miles on to Dunbar, a quaint spot that boasts its own music festival, before I swing left towards the great city will get me there. It's such an exciting prospect I can hardly sleep.

Day 16

Goodbye England and hello Scotland today. Ok, we went south to reach Southampton but since then we've headed in the right direction at a leisurely pace and waking up in Scotland this morning is definitely a landmark. Having said that, I know what lies in front of me, the confusing spaghetti bowl of major roads on the other side of Edinburgh to anyone who doesn't know the area well. Yes, I know it awaits, but now is the time to take in the breath-taking views to the right, across The Firth of Forth, across to Crail where I hoped to be sleeping off the twisty Day 17 drive, but I've changed my mind as it's all too demanding. I've always had a soft spot for Scotland, having gone to college there, but I've played the tourist card up here so I know I'll soon be venturing to pastures new the further up the country I go.

Crail is a tiny fishing village in the East Neuk of Fife, 53 miles to the east of Edinburgh surrounded by golf clubs, no surprise there. I can see it from here, across the water of The Forth, but it's a long twisty drive west and then east to get there. I have decided not to take on the busy roads of Edinburgh today. I feel I need to have a run at this place if I'm going to reach the other side in my VW camper van and make it to Crail tomorrow instead. In other words, I'm on a two-day mission to get there.

Southampton to Edinburgh taking a sensible, straight-forward route? Irrelevant. We're taking the non-straight-forward route and I need to be at my best to take on the maze that is this fine city full of personal memories. Edinburgh is a great place to lose myself for a day, especially as it gives me a chance to drive to Scotland's biggest castle, almost a town in itself. It sits on top of a burnt-out volcano and is the site of many cultural and musical events, well up my street, even though I'm not struck on bagpipes.

Driving down, or up actually, Princes Street from Waverley Station with the shops on the right, the castle is in full view, and what a monument of history it is, the most attacked castle in Europe including a failed attempt by Bonnie Prince Charlie in the 18th Century. The Pirates of The Caribbean wasn't just a movie, they were true villains of the water and 21 of them were hung here in this very castle.

The Elephant House Café, at the other end of the street, attracts thousands of visitors who flock to see where JK wrote her first Harry Potter novel, but I happen to know that isn't quite true. I know it doesn't really matter because it obviously sells lots of tea and cake for them, but her first Harry scribbles began, not in Scotland at all, but in London, in a flat above a sports shop in Clapham.

I park way up the hill, almost too steep for VW and take a stroll through the winding narrow lanes of Edinburgh that have so much history to tell to anyone who wants to listen. There is so much to see and so much to learn here and of course I have my very own memories here too, so I'll take in the history today and allow the memories to come flooding back tomorrow.

Not having any interest in politics whatsoever it saddens me to view that awful modern Parliament building and it saddens me even further that Scotland and England seem to be drifting apart. Hang on though, Scotland and England have had their disagreements for centuries, often drifting apart, so it isn't actually anything new. The only difference these days is we don't meet on battlefields and slaughter one another, a definite move forward. However, driving through England and on to Scotland, as I have, I am reminded what a stunning island we all live on and it's such a shame we can't all enjoy its beautiful scenery as one instead of arguing nine to the dozen. I'm English and I love Scotland and, equally, I'm sure there are many Scottish people who love England too, of course they do or many of them wouldn't have moved to England. It's something to think about as I get my head down without fear of meeting up with a few Scottish highlanders after my blood due to some centuries old feud. Goodnight.

Day 17

Driving north out of Edinburgh towards the airport is an eternal nightmare. I shudder to think how many passengers have missed their flights whilst being caught up in this tangle of twisted roads and tempers. The concrete spaghetti here is far more complicated than the approach to Heathrow, maybe not in the air but certainly at ground level. The queues are longer than those for the toilets at a rock festival.

The beauty here, as I leave the grand city, is the recollections of my performances at The Edinburgh Fringe Festival with my youngest daughter, Rosie, walking past the home of author Robert Louis Stevenson on our way to the theatre every day. By day we performed a kid's show at The Newtown Theatre, a stunning masonic building in St George Street, and by night, after my solo show, we hung out with other performers. Thirty-one performances in thirty-one days and thirty-one take-aways. I'd never had so many kebabs in my life, so much so that I thought I'd developed a Greek accent, plus the fact I dropped a plate in the kitchen and it smashed into a thousand pieces of Greek mosaic art. We took in all the wonderful Edinburgh sites in that month, sites I wasn't able to re-visit in total on this journey without breaking my own strict navigational rules, so I chose not to. At least I could drive through, something far more difficult, if not impossible, during the festival.

I now follow, best I can, the road-signs that take me over The Forth Bridge before heading eastward along the strip of land that resembles the back of Britain's shirt collar.

More references to football clubs now, yes more I'm afraid. This strip of land is plagued with more football clubs I have only ever heard of because they were at the bottom of my dad's football pools coupon when I was a kid. East Fife, Cowdenbeath and Dunfermline to name but three. I know nothing about any of them, they could be a team of solicitors for all I know. I'm usually made familiar with distant towns by having played at their theatres, but in this case I've drawn three blanks, as I think those three names may well do on Saturday afternoons. Anyway, it's time to change sports now, hey we're in Scotland so it doesn't leave much to the imagination.

Golfers off to St Andrews use a more direct route than the coast road I am are taking, but the A917 is a beautiful drive around Fife Ness and almost drops into the sea in places. There seems to be more golf courses here than shops and certainly more golf courses than petrol stations where I can feed the VW. Everyone around here seems to play golf, a sport that gives men their only chance to wear unbecoming white belts and for the women to wear short, pleated skirts and ridiculous sun-visors, even when it's foggy or pissing down with rain. Even those who don't play seem to have a set of clubs tucked away in a cupboard or garage. Ah yes, golf, a sport to be played by so many too unfit to indulge in other sports. They all play 18 holes, if they get that far, then they grow up, go home and dress normally for the rest of their day.

So, The Firth of Forth is to our right as we head east, taking in Kirkcaldy before we reach Leven where there is actually a porridge factory somewhere around here. If you blink you'll miss Crail and that would be a pity. It's a beautiful little village with obvious Scandinavian connections and the scene of a good few successful concerts.

I have played their Arts Festival a few times and have friends there and so it's the obvious place to share a few jars and nips. I've heard it's the smallest working fishing village harbour in Europe. I don't know if that's true but it's a long way from London's Docklands. Every time I visit Crail I go to their tiny pottery and today is no exception as I add to my collection of naïve painted works that are on sale. It's strange that I'm stuck out in the middle of nowhere and yet I'm not, it's such a friendly place. So, it's a meal at the local golf club, alcohol consumption in The Smugglers Inn and then off to bed by the side of the wide road beside the community hall until those damned seagulls start shouting at me first thing. I wonder if they squawk in a different accent to those residing in Lowestoft. A wee dram is in order I feel as I pull the curtain across the windscreen and get my slightly muzzy head down.

It has to be said the miles covered were less today than anticipated, what with negotiating that minefield of concrete veins north of Edinburgh and meeting up with friends in Crail, but not a problem as I can easily make up time tomorrow as I head in the direction of St Andrews, the very home of aforementioned golf. I will head north and then further north, so much so that much of Norway and Denmark to our right, across the sea, is falling by the wayside. I have forgotten how far north I have now travelled but it's definitely getting much colder by the day. I wouldn't be surprised to see Father Christmas and his team of reindeer at any moment. I haven't seen any snow as yet but it's up here somewhere because there are Scottish ski-resorts. That's something else I happen to know absolutely nothing about but I'm sure they don't ski across people's back gardens or driveways. No, there's definitely snow up here somewhere but it will be inland, at the tops of mountains, locations I have no intention to visit.

The sea is surprisingly calm here, nothing like the raging, crashing waves I expected. I still can't work out how I've come to perform here so many times in the last few years.

Day 18

I'm surprisingly alert this morning, the whiskey did no lasting damage to my head and I'm ready to get back on the road.

Is Britain really this huge? The simple answer is yes, 6,000 miles of coastline is a long way by anyone's standard. Venues I've played such as The Adam Smith Theatre in Kirkcaldy, The Glenfarg Folk Festival and of course Crail Community Hall are far behind me now as I finally make my way north. After such a long trek to the east I finally reach the planned destination of St Andrews. I've performed at a few posh corporate events here but never swung a club.

Yes, we all know it's the sacred home of golf, but I remember thinking St Andrews was the patron saint of indigestion, having seen the chap's name on so many tins of white powder that sent water fizzy. Hang on, what about the Scottish civil engineer, John Rennie? Didn't he have something to do with our digestive systems too? People obviously don't belch as much in Scotland as they do in England and Wales and now we know why. Perhaps the prevention of indigestion was invented in Scotland along with so many other inventions created by clever people of this canny nation.

I must be the only author who passes through St Andrews and doesn't wax lyrical about this bastion of golf. Hey there are more fish to fry I'm afraid and the only thing I choose to remember as we pass through is a small café that boasts in the window that William and Kate met there whilst having a coffee break at university. Talk about milking it, although I suppose a café has more right than most to milk anything.

Above St Andrews is another water obstacle, The River Tay. Bridges seem to be coming more to the fore the further north we travel. Ah yes, The Bridge Over The Silvery Tay, the legendary poem by William McGonnagall, a Scotsman of Irish descent who is often referred to as Scotland's worst ever poet. Scotland has an abundance of poets so he must have been pretty dreadful. The industrial looking Tay Bridge carries me over to Dundee, in the historic county of Angus, and I have immediate memories of The Caird Hall and its high ceiling where the sound seemed to disappear quicker than the audience. I seem to also recall another gig in Dryburgh but my memory is vague on this one. I have a funny feeling someone will remind me of that gig. Anyway off we go, way out east on route for Aberdeen stopping off in Arbroath, yet another football club on the east coast I know nothing about, not to mention Montrose a little further up the beach. What is my continual fixation with football clubs all about? I don't have a clue as I'm really not interested in the slightest.

I have to confess this was never my strong area as a performer and so I know little about the theatres in this area, but someone told me I couldn't visit Arbroath without sampling an Arbroath smokie. Well I have and I haven't as I've driven through without sampling their speciality. I have cold pizza to finish off instead, waste not want not. Apparently, Arbroath smokies are little haddock types that look too young to be smoking. By all accounts they have to be smoked within a 5-mile radius of the town to be authentic. Stupidly I lit the campfire 6 miles away before realising it was a complete waste of time. No I didn't, I jest.

The North Sea is much colder up here than it is down south, which probably explains why the little fish love to get in those smoking kilns and warm up their fins. It's such a shame that fish really don't have fingers or they could wear gloves and keep away from the dreaded kilns. Oh well, there's plenty more fish in the sea, well there used to be until that brutal cod war when, by all accounts from mostly drunk people, cod from Iceland came to Britain and picked on all the smaller fish like the haddock. Outrageous. To be honest I'm not sure if any of this is true but it kills brain-time as I take the coast-road up to the granite city of Aberdeen and it also proves too much whiskey can spark the imagination and there's nothing wrong with that.

The sea crashing into the rocks to our right would make a beautiful opening sequence to any movie. It's a chilly night for sure so it's into the sleeping bag a little earlier than usual. Off to Aberdeen in the morning.

Day 19

Getting on for 3 weeks behind us now and away we go again. I know it's double Dutch but I seem to have been to Aberdeen more times than I've been to Scotland. Please allow me to explain. As a support act to many rock bands in the 70s and 80s I played in Aberdeen more times than any other Scottish theatre, possibly with the exception of Glasgow. Every trip there in a tour bus took the more direct diagonal route and so this was the first time I would arrive via the coast road. Interestingly it's one of the few cities in Britain that can actually boast a beach, a pier and even its own bay, obviously named Aberdeen Bay, thus making my coastal journey there fairly easy as the road atlas is fairly self-explanatory. In 1969, the year I became a professional musician they discovered oil in The North Sea, quite possibly as a means of celebration, and Aberdeen found a new industry on which to build its wealth and build its wealth it most certainly did in the years that followed.

This journey is all about re-visiting venues I played over the years and I have already admitted this wasn't my strong area, never doing a headline concert, only supporting the big names of the rock world, but hold your horses, I haven't finished with Aberdeen yet and you're in for a bit of a surprise.

Driving through Cove Bay, just 4 miles south of the city it begins to loom in the distance. It was back in the 1700s that they began building houses with stark, grey granite from local quarries and the colour gives the place a kind of sinister appearance until you get used to it. So it's over the River Dee, and into the city.

His Majesty's Theatre is an awesome venue that attracts an audience that are well and truly up for a good time, but it wasn't the only gig I did in the area. As we head north over the bridge over yet another river, The Don, my memory takes me back to a gig I did on an oil rig, a slightly precarious oil rig that wobbled a bit. We took off from the heliport in a red and white Bristow's helicopter and flew over waves the size of London buses. It was one of those days when I didn't feel that confident that I was doing the right thing. Lots of people are prepared to die for their art and that journey was probably the closest I ever came to doing exactly that. The chopper went up and down like a yo-yo, sounding like it had failed its MOT. Some rigs are 150 miles east of Aberdeen, bobbing around in The North Sea like huge pike fishing floats. I have no idea how far we flew as I'd closed my eyes and clasped my hands together in religious fashion. The helicopter had windows, but I chose not to look out at the waves not that far below.

Needless to say, the marooned oil workers were starved of any kind of entertainment and so the show was spectacular, as was the cuisine I have to say. Someone standing on one leg bashing a tambourine would have met with thunderous applause on such a distant rig. I'm sure most people have no idea of some of the stranger places we play our music during the course of a long career. Trust me, it isn't just theatres and that oil rig is the classic example of have guitar will travel.

As I head north from the Granite City I try to spot an oil rig out in the distance, maybe the very one, but I can't see any as they are so far out to sea, so my memory bank closes down as I head for pastures new. I'm now in an area that I simply don't know, but it's a truly beautiful experience. I intend to be in Inverness by nightfall but my immediate plan today is to drive to Pennan where they filmed Local Hero, one of my favourite movies. I knew this would be one of the highlights of my entire journey around Britain. It's a 37-mile drive north from Aberdeen and we're on our way to the little fishing village with the famous red telephone box. As I say, this is somewhere I've always wanted to go and my body tingles at the very thought. It's right up on the top shoulder of Aberdeenshire and a perfect place to stop for a while and take in the beauty of Scotland before heading westward and dropping down slightly to Inverness.

One of my dreams has finally come true and you can't wipe the smile off my face with a lemon. I see Burt Lancaster and Peter Capaldi in my head, along with the admirably shaped Jenny Seagrave and the amazing music of Mark Knopfler. I don't know how many times I've watched Local Hero and I never dreamt I would one day visit the location where it was filmed. They made the film in 1983 and Pennan has hardly changed during the 40 years that have since passed.

There are flights from Southampton Airport to Inverness, just a couple of hours of sitting up in the sky doing a crossword and that very fact makes me realise yet again what I have taken on with my desire to travel Britain's coastline in 80 days on the ground, but had I flown here I would never have visited Pennan with that beautiful music ringing in my head.

The Eden Court Theatre in Inverness I played twice, with Jethro Tull and Elkie Brooks, so the previous trips there were in a luxurious Len Wright Travel tour bus and not a spluttering VW camper van, but I made it safely in time to find a place to rest up for the night.

Inverness is such a fascinating place, for example a byelaw was passed there in 1756, long before my time I should stress here, that entitled all children to obtain a free set of bagpipes on their 10th birthday. Ouch, and everyone over 10, we can assume, was presented with free earplugs. It also boasts the deepest lake in Britain, by the name of Lake Marar and 16 miles south-west is the infamous Loch Ness. I have no intention of wasting our time looking for the monster as I've always had my serious doubts. From its first sighting I worked out the thing would be 110 years old by now, an inaccuracy as you're about to read, but it's probably trolling along the bottom of the loch in a wheelchair or on crutches.

Despite having said all that, I have still decided to stay the night by the banks of this famous loch, further on than my original plan to stay in beautiful Inverness. Quite a few other motorhomes seem to have had the same idea, or at least their owners have. It resembles a small folk festival site and I think I'm the only man here who doesn't have a beard or a pewter tankard. I bought a local paper to see if there was any live music in the area tonight, maybe a friendly little folk club where I could get up and play on a borrowed guitar, but sadly there was no such gig, a shame as it seemed just that kind of a place and my fingers are itchy.

All the motorhomes parked by the bankside are in a long line and my weary VW camper van looks very much the poor relation, or so I thought. It may look it, but it certainly isn't, it's more a surviving status symbol of freedom as people knew it in the 1960s and 1970s and so it has a kind of pride of place. It has no reason to feel inferior, just because it hasn't got a shower or a toilet like the bigger boys. I've lined it up alongside the rest of them and I feel proud because other campers are admiring my mechanical friend at close range.

As I prepare to settle down for the night I eat my words slightly as a bearded gentlemen plonks himself down outside his caravan and starts playing a couple of tunes on a concertina, or an acoustic armadillo as I tend to call them. A small crowd has gathered and suddenly we're all singing the chorus to Will Ye Go Lassie Go.

The power of music never ceases to amaze me and it's something the government didn't take into account during the recent lockdown when us professional musicians were all told to go out and find other jobs. They got it so wrong because they seriously under-valued the need for music and entertainment at a time of great stress and this, at Loch Ness, was the proof. One moment we were a bunch of strangers on the banks of a sight-seeing loch and the next, through music, we had become a friendly community, laughing, singing and passing round cans of beer. The smell of sausages on the barbecue fills the air as we sing traditional Scottish songs, even if we don't know the words. It's a rare contact with people for me, particularly strangers whom I never knew in past visits to the various areas I have planned. It's all quite enlightening and it couldn't happen in a more unspoilt part of Britain, apart from us sightseers and the gift shops dotted around the place, but you know what I mean. A most delightful evening that pushed back the years for me. I don't remember the last time I sang The Wild Rover but I bellowed it out at the top of my voice. I may well be a professional musician, but that remains a secret tonight because it doesn't matter. Sometimes music is more important than the quality of its performance and if they'd discovered I do it for a living it would probably have made them a little uncertain and that would have killed the moment stone dead. If that monster was lurking in the depths of the loch then you can bet your life it was tapping its flippers to the rhythm of our efforts.

Day 20

Everyone seems to be up bright and early this morning. We're all waving and chatting as a result of last night's impromptu music session. Some of my new-found friends have already set off in boats in search of the nasty beastie, binoculars hanging from their necks and cameras at the ready. As someone just said to me, there's more chance of a one-legged man winning an arse-kicking contest, but I wish them all luck just the same.

The café by the loch is very busy this morning, selling wonderful hearty Scottish breakfasts and little monsters on which to hang your car-keys. Where to now I ask myself. Go north young man, go north. The problem is it's hard to drag myself away from such a truly beautiful spot and new friends I have met and every time I think about moving on I meet yet another really interesting character, each with their own facts and theories about this mystical place.

Despite my previous plan to move on to pastures new I've decided to spend another day here and relax as I can't really think of anywhere nicer I would wish to be right now and a rest from driving for a day would be very welcome.

I have learnt so much about Loch Ness from the locals here. It's nearly 800 feet deep in places and 23 miles long, so those hopefuls may well need more than a pair of binoculars, especially as beneath the surface it's more or less pitch black. It's second only in size to Loch Lomond and that's quite a boast when you discover there are 32,000 lochs in Scotland. There are so many interesting and highly intelligent people around me and all as one believe there is a monster lurking somewhere under the water. Maybe they're right and maybe I have got it so wrong after all.

There are also conflicting guesses of the monster's age too. If you recall I mentioned I may have guessed its age wrong at 110 years of age, and here is the reason I have my doubts. According to a Myths and Legends book I purchased at the café, the first sighting was by St Columba, back in 565AD, when, by all accounts or should I say this account in particular, the thing tried to eat one of his servants. If it's true we have a very old monster on our hands and definitely not a vegetarian. I doubt its existence even more now but it's still all so magical.

It all goes to prove that alcohol is a fine drink that can confuse the mind if too much passes the lips. Speaking of which, it would be remiss of me not to sit by the banks of this amazing stretch of water and not enjoy a wee dram before I enter the land of dreams later tonight. My lingering memory of my second day here? A little lad in the gift shop trying to get his dad to buy him a fishing rod and the excited, bubbly little boy asking the shopkeeper to suggest the best bait to catch Nessie. Sadly my little friend, it would have taken more than a wriggling worm, but the legend lives on in the mind of the youngster and that's gratifying.

As I think about it today I have been taken in by the mystique of this wonderful spot. I'm not sure if there's a monster swimming around down there without daring to show its head above the water and yet it's possible existence, possible but highly unlikely, helps to make this somewhere very special. It must be because I have given the place an extra day when I should have been back on the road. I suppose it's no different to Robin Hood and his merry men living in Sherwood

Forest is it? We all just go with it without a single shrug of the shoulder. That's the beauty of folklore, so many of our British folksongs tell stories of legendary characters who probably didn't exist but it doesn't dilute the values of our folk tradition. Yes, I get it all and more so since I took on this massive journey.

Day 21

Today is the 3-week landmark. With the wildness of The Moray Firth to my right I negotiate three small bridges that didn't have nameplates as I enter the county of Sutherland, on the A9, before joining the coast road once again a little further to the north, passing through the delightful seaside resort of Dornoch, a Gaelic word for Pebbly Place, a strange name as the beach here is absolutely stunning. Nondurnoch may have been more suitable.

Interesting but irrelevant, in 2000 Madonna had her son Rocco christened in Dornoch Cathedral the day before she married film producer Guy Ritchie in a nearby castle. I only know that because they still talk about it to gullible visitors such as myself who are prepared to, and have the time to, listen. Apparently Madonna once nearly bought a house near me. Apparently Madonna nearly bought a house near everyone in the country. What is it that seems to be so magnetic about that lady?

It's a kind of north-easterly journey now as we head upwards to the very roof of Britain and the land seems to stretch that way towards, err, The Shetlands or even Iceland I suppose. No idea. For your information we are exactly 600 miles from London by a more direct route than mine, which is actually even more pointless information and I don't know why I bother to keep mentioning it. I must have given a few dozen or more direct route updates in the last couple of weeks and I can't for the life of me think why. It's probably because I'd mapped out the route and distances in Salisbury before setting off, never thinking it would be such a complete waste of time and exceedingly boring to boot. Hey, the planning was all part of the excitement so I make no apologies. I spent so many winter evenings with my road atlas and a glass of wine deciding how I would undertake this project and where I would go, but it was obvious things wouldn't go quite to plan.

My plan today is to reach Smoo Cave up near Durness, a place I'd read about somewhere or other and a place well worth a visit in the North-West Highlands. Its entrance is almost rectangular, 50 feet high and 130 feet wide, wow, it's so impressive. It's also 200 feet long. A noisy waterfall drops around 70 or 80 feet into a deep waterhole and it was well worth a stop off as I've never witnessed anything like this before. It's like something from a movie.

I arrived at Durness after a sweeping drive from a north-east to a westerly direction at the very tip of our great island, by-passing Thurso town to visit smaller places along the coast. Dunnet Bay was bigger than I expected to my right on the A836, as was Thurso Bay. It's odd that we think of bays as small and then, when we get up close, most of them are monstrous in size, just like our grandparents or school headmasters.

I filled the van up with juice in Scrabster and not many people can say that. As I headed west, towards Durness and the cave, I suddenly realised I'd been just about as high as I could go without taking in islands too difficult to navigate, and now I seem to be slightly edging back south. Honestly, I'm so far north I feel like I could bang my head on some remote island, of which there are many up here. Perhaps I have finally reached an important landmark of my journey. The coastline along our island's roof is absolutely beautiful, ooo, I've just seen a sign for The Ness of Litter. Well, perhaps they should tidy the place up then. Great name.

The roads are narrow and twisty and I haven't covered the miles I had planned today but, as I've stated many times before, it really doesn't matter. It's a pleasure to just toodle along at the speed of a gaping tourist and take in the glorious scenery along with the mighty Atlantic Ocean roaring away to my right. I must admit, as I mentioned in Edinburgh, I don't follow politics, especially Scottish politics, but I have to say this is all a far cry from Westminster. No wonder they have their doubts. I think I would if I lived up this way. The Scottish folk scene has songs of rebellion and revolution, always has done, and I can see why. Throughout history there must have been more island gate-crashing here than anywhere else in Britain and I now know it wasn't just The Romans who turned up uninvited.

It's time to park up for the night with weary legs and arms that did more clutch work and gear-changing than expected today. So where are we now? We have been somewhere adjacent to the Kyle of Tongue. I passed through the village of Skerray earlier and I peered over Rabbits Island before making it to Durness. There are so many signposts to take in here I seem to be getting giddy trying to read them all as I drive by. It's so ruggedly beautiful but my eyes are sore. So many beauty spots I have never seen before or will ever see again.

I'm not totally sure where I am now because I've taken refuge in a small forest in the middle of nowhere but I'm perfectly happy. The smell of pine is stronger than anything you could hang from your rear-view mirror. I'll try to make sense of it all tomorrow but right now I'm lost in a new world that I knew nothing about, shame upon me. I've been in and out, up and down, uphill and down dale for the whole day and it's left me drained but very content.

Tomorrow we will head for Cape Wrath, the very top. I have a sense of reaching the top of Mount Everest such is my adulation of getting here. What's at Cape Wrath? An awful lot of Atlantic Ocean I reckon, but right now I don't know much more than that. It will be so exciting to find out. I've never done a show anywhere near here, I doubt if few people ever have, but I must admit I would have loved to have given it a bash. Time for shut eye.

Day 22

So off we go to Cape Wrath, the turning point of our trip around Britain because it's the northernmost part of our journey before the VW begins its journey back down to the more familiar south.

Well, it isn't exactly a motorway, thank God for that, but we made it. Well we sort of made it because I never realised that Cape Wrath is actually an island separated from the mainland by The Kyle of Durness. It has a white lighthouse reaching out above a cliff, but I know little more than that. I've never seen so many walkers with their long, woolly orange socks and heavy rucksacks, there are dozens and dozens of them, like a herd of rarely seen animals.

Durness is still the closest place, just 10 miles away and Inverness is just 120 miles although it seems a darn sight longer after the last 24 hours of driving. No-one seems to live here other than a fair number of sheep so surely it must at least boast a shepherd or two. Yes, surely a shepherd lives somewhere around here.

We are still in the Scottish county of Sutherland, but the time has come to begin our journey downwards, dare I say to more civilisation as I know it. Aha, I spot a Ministry of Defence sign which gives me some kind of clue as to what goes on at Cape Wrath and why few people populate the area. Time to head on as I'm not particularly interested in that kind of thing. It's all a little too sinister for me.

My lasting memory of Cape Wrath is barbed wire with little pieces of white wool attached at various intervals where the sheep scratched their backs or accidentally collided with the nasty form of fencing.

I'm supposed to be heading for Fort William, quite a drive, but I'm distracted by a cluster of islands to my right, The Outer Hebrides, The Uists North and South and The Isle of Skye. The decision is made to spend some time island hopping. To an ignorant Englishman such as myself I envisage such islands as being not that big. Oh really? Beginning with The Outer Hebrides, it's 130 miles long and is made up of 220 islands of which 15 are inhabited. Below them is North Uist where, believe it or not, I once did a gig, a most memorable gig because it was day of Princess Diana's funeral, 6th September 1997. Actually the gig was a short hop from North Uist to Benbecula and what I remember most about the place was its population of albino hedgehogs.

Below and to the right of the Uists is Skye, part of the Inner Hebrides and probably one of the most famous islands alongside The Shetlands, an outpost which, along with Orkney, I never reached on this trip around a mainland coastline in the main. I did diversify and change the rules later but Shetland, a fair distance away, really was pushing it.

To take in such west-coast outposts meant I wouldn't make Fort William as planned. In fact I knew I wouldn't even make it back to the mainland, but I have decided the diversion will be well worth it. Their magnitude is somewhat surprising with Skye being 692 square miles, 8 times bigger than The Isle of Wight, The Outer Hebrides, taking in Lewis and Harris is 741 square miles and North Uist is 334 square miles. That's nearly 2,000 square miles around these islands, but some of those miles have to be done. It's so wildly exhilarating. There are so many wonderful fiddle players up here too so I hope to hear one or two whilst I'm here.

It takes two days to take it all in and it's all far more confusing than I thought it would be. By plane it's so easy, but on land and ferry it's a different matter.

Although nothing to do with where we are today, the shortest flight in Britain is also the shortest flight in the whole world and it happens up here in Scotland between the two Orkney Islands of Westray and Papa Westray. The flight is under two miles and takes as little as 45 seconds, depending of course on the weather. No movies then. It's a far cry from here and well worthy of a mention, but now we return to the west of Scotland islands and the matters in hand.

In simple terms I have made my way south, down the islands of The Outer Hebrides before heading back inland a little to The Isle of Skye at the bottom of the other islands. Have I ever performed up here, you sarcastically ask? You'll be surprised to know the answer is yes. London corporate company, Production Plus, booked me to appear on The Isle of Islay when Bells Distillery launched a new brand of whiskey. I don't remember too much about the gig, for obvious reasons, but I seem to recall the flight from Glasgow on the Scottish mainland was so short I sneezed and missed the take-off and landing. It wasn't as short as The Orkney Islands hop but it wasn't too far short.

It's all been somewhat confusing. Under normal circumstances I would stay strictly to the coastline and by-pass islands, just like I had with regards The Shetlands and The Orkney Islands, but there's nothing wrong with making exceptions to the rule If I see fit when I'm not sure exactly what constitutes part of the coastline. I would make further exceptions when I reach Anglesey, The Isles of Scilly and The Isle of Wight. Come to think of it, in a less obtrusive way, I did the same just a few days into the venture when I hopped over to Canvey Island from the Essex coast, so there have been no hard and fast rules, just whatever takes me fancy as I arrive at a certain part of Britain.

Day 23

That being explained, I'm not sure if this day constitutes part of the drive around Britain's main coastline or not, mainly because I'm not sure, as I also mentioned, what is and what isn't considered the main coastline here. There are so many islands, almost enough to spread over a prawn cocktail, along with bridges and ferries, making it all far too confusing to work out. It's a bit like wondering if your beard is part of your hair or your toes are part of your legs, the sort of ponders that keep you awake at night. In my defence though, how can you possibly come to such a wonderful unspoilt part of Britain and not have a good look around? It just wouldn't feel right.

In a nutshell, I'm not sure where I am or where I'm going today but I so wish I had brought my watercolour paints with me. The scenery is breath-taking and inspiring. This is definitely a toodle and a doodle day if ever there was one, a day of totally confused enjoyment.

I think this may well be the appropriate time to sing the praises of dear old VW, the VW camper van, who has answered the call admirably despite its age, something we have in common. It has negotiated the ragged up and down Scottish coastline without complaint, slowing up to admire the scenery every so often, not by choice but slowing down just the same. The gearbox made a few grunts of despair at times but nothing to warrant a complete mental or mechanical breakdown. You may have already noticed it's VW when I'm being affectionate, as that's its name, or VW camper van when I'm being more matter of factual. They are not grammatical errors, just a freedom of choice in a modern world where freedom of choices are rare commodities. I remember a time when everyone gave their vehicles names, usually female, a tradition that has died with car-leasing and HP agreements. They're not our friends anymore, just things the get us from a to b in a hurry.

It's really funny to see how people still respect VW camper vans though. It's not unusual for other motorists in faster cars to curse the slower drivers who hold them up, we all see it a hundred times a day, but it's never the case with those stuck behind my friend. It seems to be a kind of understanding whereby drivers appreciate it's going as fast as it can go and can't be hurried. In return, VW camper van drivers respect those who want to travel faster and get somewhere quicker, maybe to work or to an important meeting, so they never hog a middle or outside lane. They just stay in the inside lane with the trucks and nervous drivers whose noses stick to the windscreens and not get done for speeding. One thing's for sure, if you need to get your skates on and drive to an important meeting you definitely don't use a VW camper van. Let me expand upon this equal respect thing.

As I said, we all get annoyed with stupidly slow drivers who hog the wrong lanes of motorways and it's a fact that they can cause more accidents, particularly involving lorries, than faster cars trying to win The British Grand Prix in the outside lane. You never see a VW camper van behaving like that do you? No, they always tuck themselves into that slow lane and mind their own business. You seldom see one in a multiple pile-up and never do you see one of them shunting another vehicle up the backside, so yes, the respect is mutual. However, the one thing you do see is one camper van owner waving to another, they being members of a very exclusive, clandestine club. A bit like the VW Beetle, they are respected vehicles that annoy no-one. AA patrolmen used to do the same friendly gesture, saluting to a member coming the other way if that member had an AA badge on their radiator. Nowadays, as far as the AA are concerned, it takes three different breakdown trucks to get you home when things go mechanically wrong. Those patrolmen didn't have cars but motorbikes with a yellow sidecar full of tools.

The very first VW camper van was launched at The Geneva Motor Show way back in 1949, the year I was also born so another thing we have in common. Most of the models that have managed to survive to this day were on the forecourts the following year and they were known as The Microbus. In 1951, forever modernising the design, the manufacturers added a deeper dashboard that could accommodate a road atlas without it slipping off, along with a radio. A radio in a vehicle? Yes, a radio in a vehicle, despite the lack of radio stations. Back-to-back music programmes didn't exist but there many comedy programmes, gardening programmes and numerous quizzes to keep us occupied. Camper vans were built to travel on the narrow roads of the time and certainly not the aggressive motorways that would follow later, and that may well be why our very own camper van has performed so well so far on this journey. It feels in its element, back to how things used to be, safe and unaffected by bigger, faster roads.

No other motorists have been annoyed with us on our entire journey and it's because they know they can't hurry us, so there's little point. Camper van drivers are chilled-out characters who aren't concerned with speed or temper. Yes, they're all going somewhere, just like we are up here in

Scotland, but they're not that bothered what time they arrive, just like us, so long as they get there in time to pitch up before darkness, that's what suits a camper van driver.

The Western Isles of Scotland are subject to drastic variations in weather, but lady luck has been on my side today as all is calm.

Day 24

In simple terms I block the isles of The Outer Hebrides into three. Yes, very simplistic terms, and, yesterday, I began up on the Isle of Lewis and Harris and worked my way down before visiting Skye. You cannot help but be on a coast road on Lewis and the other islands as you have no choice. Starting out from Stornoway I drove up to The Butt of Lewis, the windiest place in Britain by all accounts and Port Ness, jutting out in The North Atlantic. The lighthouse here used to operate by the burning of fish oil until they adapted to the more modern fuel of paraffin in 1862. There's a plaque on its wall that boasts its remarkable history so I know it's true.

It was a dead-end road to the northern tip and so I took a look around before turning back south towards Callanish and Achmore. By the time I reached Harris, to the south of the island and home of the famous Harris tweed, I was ready for a rest and thus I welcomed the ferry trip at Tarbert. Taking in such stunning views was actually really tiring, and there was more of the same to follow.

If, like me, you've listened to those weather forecasts on the radio and wondered where the hell the named places were, then I can inform you that Rockall is about 230 miles west of this area of Scotland. Useful to know if you win the lottery and buy yourself a boat but a pointless fact to know if you fancy yourself as a half-decent swimmer.

By the end of the day I have done my duty and paid my respects to a most beautiful part of Scotland. It's such a shame I couldn't find a pub with live music going on, but maybe that's just how I imagined this area in my head. My second day of being lost in a most perfect wilderness has now drawn to a close with the most amazing sunset. It must be both a hard and simple way of life over here and I must admit to pangs of envy as I see the isolated crofter's cottages. I'd swap tomorrow given half the chance. Speaking of tomorrow . . .

Day 25

Ok, let's have a second attempt at making Fort William but this time we'll travel further south once we get there as we need to make up time after my 2-day diversion to the beautiful islands.

It's goodbye to the rugged Scottish islands with another couple of hundred miles under our belt. Let me tell you, on the ferry back to the mainland you really can't get that Skye Boat song out of your head. It's an earworm of great magnitude not helped by others whistling it on the bloody ferry too. How quickly such a beautiful ballad can turn into a total annoyance through no fault of its own. Fort William is a return to modern civilisation in so many different ways.

Fort William was named after William of Orange, apparently a name that won the vote over Billy Fruit. It was originally nothing more than a wooden fort they built in 1654, just a bigger version than the wooden things you buy at garden centres. With the population it now has they obviously built an extension or two. We are now in Cameron clan country by the way.

I choose not to hang around in Fort William as there is catching up to be done after the island hopping and it's a fairly straightforward journey south from Fort William down to Oban and at last a theatre I once played, The Oban Theatre funnily enough. I don't recall them being packed in like sardines but I'm sure they had a good time, hope so anyway. The distance from Fort William to Oban is around 45 miles, but it will probably end up more by the time I've wriggled along the coastline and stopped off for a hearty lunch.

When arriving in Oban the island of Mull is to our right. For some reason, Paul McCartney springs to mind as he may well to you too. I remember him standing windswept on some windy hill singing that song in 1977 next to guitarist Denny Laine and being more than surprised when a band of pipers take over. Apparently when standing on Mull the Northern Irish coast can be seen in the distance, not that we would sadly ever find out for ourselves.

Day 26

We could easily take the M9 motorway to Stirling, but that would be cheating and definitely not as much fun. Despite that I still plan to cover another 100 miles today, a distance that would indeed see us arrive in Stirling.

Driving through Oban and out the other side Scotland splinters into various fingers of land, far too difficult to negotiate in the camper van, but today is a straightforward drive to Stirling Is there a nice theatre in Stirling? There most certainly is but for the life of me its name escapes me, sorry Stirling.

It's said that there are over 2,000 castles in Scotland and Stirling Castle ranks as one its grandest. You can't help but have it in your sights as you drive through the comparatively small market town. The area was built around the twisty River Forth and various historic characters are linked to the castle. Bonnie Prince Charlie had a bash at taking it and failed and Mary Queen of Scots came to prominence there too.

It's really strange that Stirling isn't exactly a massive place but it seems huge, almost endless, compared to the small villages and windswept hamlets we drove through over the last 3 days. That said, it will be a true eye-opener when we hit Glasgow tomorrow. I look forward to that kind of homecoming as I went to college in Glasgow and so many memories are bound to come flooding back. I find parking area at the end of Dumbarton Road and manage to find a fish and chip just down the road. I decide to have a mini banquet in the back of the VW, a proper sit-down meal, so excited that I will be making my way to my old student haunt in the morning. I try to work out the mileage but it seems to be more complicated by the day, so let's just say 2,500 miles, that's close enough, especially as it doesn't really matter so long as I make it back to Southampton by the time day 80 comes along. After consuming a nice piece of fresh haddock and chips that haven't been swimming in oil for days, I go to sleep on a full stomach and happy heart. As my eyes begin to close I smile at a joke I once heard. Can you name three Grand Prix racing drivers whose surnames are Scottish towns? Stirling, Hamilton and Ayr Town Centre, boom boom. I'll get my coat and I'll see you in the morning.

Day 27

Stirling to Glasgow is under 30 miles but I have a hunch I will be well below my predicted mileage today. As I leave my overnight car park I turn right and make my way over to the coast once again via the A811, passing through the village of Kippen on the way to Dumbarton. The sea is on our right once again as I swing to the left and drive to Milngavie to the north of Glasgow. I'm not cheating as The River Clyde runs to the south of me at this point.

I know the district of Milngavie well as it's the home of a folk club held in The Fraser Centre. I've played there a couple of times in recent years and suddenly, something is finally looking far more familiar than The Western Isles, something I haven't been able to say since I drove out of Inverness a good few days ago.

I lived in Glasgow for a while, in the district of Shawlands, but it would be a complete maze for me to find my way through the chaos from the northwest down to Shawlands, 2 miles south of The River Clyde. The river has widened enough here to consider it to be part of the coastline and so, using some poetic licence, I'm through the city and out the other side, just like I did in Newcastle, before veering right to find the 'official' coast once again in the opposite direction to where I once lived in Minard Road. It would have been nice to have taken a look at my old stomping ground but it wasn't possible on this occasion.

I have performed in Glasgow more times than I can recount here without boring you, quite literally dozens of times, but I should perhaps give mention to The Glasgow Folk

Centre in Montrose Street, my first ever visit to a folk club, and of course The Glasgow Apollo where I performed many times during the 1970s and 1980s as a support act to the top rock bands. There, I've indeed given mention but none of these venues will be in view today, so enough said.

It's all very well but I need to get back out to the countryside and continue my journey south, eventually at least, because I need to drive north-ish again to negotiate the peninsula past the airport as I travel on my way to Largs on the A78.

As a matter of interest, if you were to draw a straight horizontal line from Largs in the west across Scotland you would discover it's dead in line with Berwick on Tweed in the east, and the width of Scotland at this point is just 133 miles. It's easy to forget how narrow Scotland is at this point. Yes I know what you're thinking, wouldn't it have been far easier to have driven across to Glasgow from Berwick Upon Tweed. Yes of course but that wasn't the idea at all. When you think about it, I could have driven from West Southampton across to East Southampton on Day 1 and not bothered to do any of this if that had been the case.

Once again Scotland splits into numerous fingers here, very much a familiar picture of the west of Scotland further north. Before reaching Largs I pull over at Greenock to take a look across the water to Dunoon on the Cowal Peninsula where I performed at the Dunoon Folk Festival back in the late 1960s, a special weekend where I met Billy Connolly. Funnily enough, despite being on the same scene and on the same record label I never met him again. That said, he was amazing to watch and remains a big influence.

I'm sure Dunoon welcomed that folk festival and that seemed to be confirmed as I stared across to the place and remembered how so many American Marines strolled around. Yes, it was very much a military garrison and I have to wonder what they made of a few hundred hippies turning up with their acoustic guitars and ban the bomb slogans. It's a roundabout way of heading south but now we're on our way down to Troon, by-passing Kilmarnock on our left. It's a sharp left turn at The Firth of Clyde or the VW would need to turn into an amphibious craft.

It's the final drive through Scotland, along the Solway Firth, as I steer my way towards Gretna Green, the famous town in the county of Dumfries and Galloway. Couples used to elope there to be married at the blacksmith's, replacing a church altar for an anvil. It seems a good place to fall asleep tonight, in the town where so many newly-weds spent their very own wedding nights presumably not falling asleep like tired old me.

Purely out of interest, do couples still marry at Gretna Green? Yes is the answer but unlike many years ago you can't just turn up and tie the knot straight away. It can take 30 days for all the admin to be done in this wonderful modern world we now live in. I wonder if there's a place that offers a similar drive-in service for divorces. Blimey, that would have saved me a small fortune.

My journey around Scotland is drawing to a close now as tomorrow we cross back over the border to England. I so enjoyed the coastal jaunt around Scotland, particularly my visit to Pennan, Local Hero land, and of course my return to my college days in Glasgow. Then of course there was Edinburgh and my drive up the east coast and round to Loch Ness. I really have seen so much in the last few days, so much so that I shall feel a gulp as I wave goodbye to Scotland, a country I have re-discovered and become quite attached to. The driving will be considerably easier now as the coastline becomes more obvious tomorrow.

I shall sleep well tonight.

Day 28

Good morning, it's time to travel to England. I began this journey around Britain exactly 4 weeks ago but I still have a fair way to go before I get back to Southampton, and I must admit, I'm in no real hurry.

It was only this morning, when I checked the page of my road atlas, that I realised that I travelled decidedly upwards as opposed to downwards to get to Gretna. The other thing I realised is, despite how much Scotland and England seem to be at verbal war with each other, it's nothing new. We seem to have been at each other's throats for centuries, 2,000 Scottish castles are confirmation of that, and being the peace-loving hippie that I am, I think it's a shame. No doubt I'll find a similar historic scenario when I arrive in Wales in days to follow. There's no doubt about it, the English haven't always been welcome visitors to other countries through the years. And I'm not just talking about our island as we were hostile intruders when we built The British Empire too in various countries around the world, making them learn how to play cricket. It's so true when you think about it. I struggle to think of a country outside of the former Empire or Commonwealth that plays cricket, proving those who had a choice didn't bother. Let's face it, who would volunteer to play a game that lasts 5 days and usually ends in a draw? Cricket was invented so the English could tour warmer climes and get away from the drab weather at home, so long as they won.

The sign by the side of the road says, 'Welcome to England' and after the last paragraph I'm quite pleased I managed to get back unscathed. The short journey from Gretna to Carlisle takes just over 15 minutes. As we all know, Carlisle is where Hadrian's bricklayers got to work, building a wall between England and Scotland 14 miles south of the border. I think he got something wrong there, but there again he probably didn't have a road atlas like I have.

Although I've driven past the place a good few times I'd only been into Carlisle centre once before, to play The Brewery Arts Centre. I couldn't have gone down too well or they would have surely booked me back, which they didn't. It was so long ago I couldn't stir my memory, so it was straight through with no hanging around. We hug the coastline again as we drive the 33 miles of the A596, through Wigton and Maryport, to Workington. It takes us in a sort of south-westerly direction and if we continued in a straight line we'd glide across The Irish Sea and crash headlong into The Isle of Man, not a particularly great idea as the island seems to have enough crashes of its own, albeit of the two-wheel variety.

Excuse my ignorance but I never knew until today that The Isle of Man is not part of The United Kingdom and never has been. I'm sure you knew that, but I have to admit that I didn't. It doesn't have any representation at Westminster and it's not part of the EU either, so I didn't need to even contemplate driving around it as it's out of bounds. In other words, The Isle of Man is its own boss and I like that as I'm my own boss too.

I've played The Gaiety Theatre 3 times and sat on a bench outside the nearby Sefton Hotel, next to a statue of Sir Norman Wisdom, so I thought about sailing over there when I originally planned this trip, but I now realise it would be totally irrelevant. Anyway, where was I?

As I begin to circumnavigate The Lake District I soon realise how well I know this part of the Cumbrian coastline well. The coastal town of Workington has a theatre with the splendorous name of The Carnegie, thus making me think it's somewhat misplaced and should be in America, but no. In 1904, Scotsman Andrew Carnegie donated £7,500 to build it and so he deserved the namecheck. I played there twice.

Continuing along the coast a further 8 miles we arrive in Whitehaven, home of The Rosehill Theatre. South of the Marina, Whitehaven sticks out into the sea a little, not unlike a sore thumb or a boil on the end of your nose, before levelling out once more.

My final theatre memory tour of Cumbria will end at The Forum Theatre in Barrow in Furness, a further 48 miles down the western coastline. Barrow is nestled in Morecambe Bay and was historically part of Lancashire before being taken in by Cumbria. They used to make ships here for The British Navy but that was long ago. Once again it's a journey east, taking the A5092 to Kirby in Furness before heading onwards to Grange Over Sands where I have decided to spend the night.

I knew nothing about the place but when I arrived I was captivated by its cosiness. I reckon it used to be a tiny fishing village years ago but there's not much sign of that now. If I'd driven 7 miles inland I could have spent the night on the banks of Lake Windermere, the stretch of water where William Wordsworth used to live in Dove Cottage, but I had to keep true to my plan and stay by the coast. Grange Over Sands is so peaceful and relaxing, the perfect place to take a rest before taking on the brain-bashing onslaught of glitzy Blackpool tomorrow.

Many will say The Lake District is the most beautiful part of England and they may well be right. Back in the day folksingers would do Lake District tours, taking in the small villages of Egremont, The Salutation at Windermere and Kendall. A great way to spend a week. So many villages had their own folk clubs as it was easier than travelling to a town, miles away, to watch a show. It was always part of the deal to be given a bed for the night at these places and thus many lasting friendships were made. On this journey I have literally swept around the perimeter of The Lakes and therefore wasn't able to re-visit old haunts, but they stay in my memory just the same. I must have done 5,000 or more shows around Britain, averaging about 100 per year.

I often wonder what happened to all the nice people I met along the way. I wouldn't be at all surprised if some of them didn't retire here, to The Lake District, for a quieter, slower life. I bump into a few every so often but not as many as I would like. Yes, I remember The Lake District well and the memories of shows still linger. A PA system? What the hell was a PA system? Village halls didn't even have locks on their doors or fire exits, let alone PA systems. I can only assume that I must have sung much louder and bashed my guitar harder back in the day.

Day 29

Talk about chalk and cheese. I leave behind the tranquillity of Cumbria as today I prepare myself for the drive down to sunny Blackpool, the home of summer seasons for stand-up comedians. It's a journey of round about 50 miles but I sense there will be a few stops along the way. The dreaded M6 motorway is to my left but no thank you very much. I hate that road as much as I hate indigestion in the middle of the night.

Morecambe is a place I know nothing about other than the fact that comedian Eric Bartholomew was born there in 1926 and changed his name to that of the town. I pay my respects to the great man's statue as I drive through the town, none the wiser really.

However, just below Morecambe is the more familiar Heysham where I used to catch a ferry when I did short tours of the banned, out of bounds Isle of Man. It was always a bit of a bumpy crossing despite the short journey.

And then there was Fleetwood Folk Club, a nice gig and one of the oldest folk clubs in the country, so it all came flooding back to me as I headed, reluctantly I have to admit, for the land of candyfloss and sticks of rock.

My first trip to Blackpool was to play at their folk club, run by The Blackpool Taverners at the now flattened Kings Arms, but in later years I performed at The Opera House and did a few corporate gigs at The Imperial Hotel on the promenade. However, my first ever encounter with Blackpool was within the pages of Charles Buchan's Football Monthly where I saw a photograph of our greatest ever footballer, Sir

Stanley Matthews. Strangely I still think of everyone walking around Blackpool in tangerine football shirts and cowboy hats. I know that's unfair but that's nostalgia for you, a misconception of things still being the way they were when you were a kid. I have to confess that I could say the same about Southend and even Great Yarmouth to a certain extent.

I must also confess that Blackpool isn't really my kind of place as I always found donkey rides cruel and I have no idea why the tower was put up in the first place although it must help mobile-phone signals, so after spending what seemed an eternity to get through the town of flashing lights, arcades and trams, I welcomed the eventual peace and quiet of Lytham St Annes.

They have a lovely acoustic music club at The Pavilion in the ornamental gardens where I've performed twice over the last couple of years. Before then I used to play at The Lowther Pavilion, further in towards the town, so yes I played Lytham St Annes more often than much bigger Blackpool, and, additionally, there's also a tasty fish and chip mobile restaurant by the car park that swings round and juts out into the sea along from The Pavilion. This is an ornamental part of the coast and so it seems like the perfect place to hang out through the hours of darkness, so why not.

I definitely haven't covered the anticipated mileage today but I seem to have been driving forever and my weary head needs to recover from all the razmataz.

All is quiet in this backwater part of Lancashire as I start to doze, but I can't help thinking about the din and mayhem just down the road, the sound of slot machines in the arcades and drunk girls on hen do's wearing stupid pink cowboy hats and little else in the town I left behind a short time ago. It may well be a stereotypical description of Blackpool, but it's what I've experienced through the years. To think they had a lovely quaint folk club right outside Blackpool Station years ago. Now, having been demolished, it's just a memory to both me and the folk music loving public of Blackpool.

Day 30

I need to get my skates on if I am to complete my journey around Britain in 80 days. My plan has fallen by the wayside somewhat since I hit Lancashire, long before that to be honest, and it's time to forget about various distractions as I have done on various locations and make my way further south with greater haste.

Today my plan is to reach Liverpool, drive out the other side, as I tend today when I reach the bigger places, and circumnavigate The Wirral before heading downstream. It's only 56 miles from Blackpool to Liverpool but it isn't really as simple as that as I'm sure you can imagine. It certainly doesn't tell the whole story of the day ahead.

Firstly, we need to head east, halfway to inland Preston, home of The Guildhall and a folk club at The Tickled Trout, to negotiate the estuary that becomes The River Ribble before heading back on ourselves, taking the coastal route to Southport, home of The Floral Hall that I must have played half a dozen times in my career. All I remember about The Floral Hall is that it used to have bright pink seats that gave me a headache. Nowadays there's a far more suitable venue here at The Atkinson. It's a fantastic facility that's designed with different-sized rooms depending upon the pulling-power of the performers. My highly enjoyable performance at The Atkinson made up for the three times I didn't do such great business at The Floral Hall.

On my way from Blackpool to Liverpool, for the first time since Glasgow, I've had to encounter irate, short-fused motorists who have no time for an ancient VW camper van that's going as fast as it can. They're all overheating, as is my VW camper van. People drive very fast in this part of the country, especially those who drive white vans a bit like dodgem cars at a fairground, so I need to have my wits about me to keep myself and my van safe from harm.

If Blackpool boasts a fairly working-class promenade, nothing wrong with that of course says the boy from East Ham, then Southport is far more discerning. I don't know the area too well but I sense it's where the successful people of Liverpool seem to buy their bigger houses. Am I wrong? Then I apologise, not profusely but I apologise just the same. The sizes of the houses here, along the coastline, happen to make me come to such a conclusion.

Liverpool is a very special place for a musician such as myself for very obvious reasons and I'm excited as I pass the venue that houses the Maghull Folk Club on my left and continue through Bootle towards the magical centre of music. Of course I've performed in the city many times myself, The Liverpool Empire I remember being the major concert hall where I stood and gaped so often at the size of the crowd. Behind the Empire is The Central Hotel that used to be the home of Liverpool Folk Club and yes, of course I would have given my back teeth to have strummed my guitar at The Cavern Club while Cilla Black flogged the tickets.

The River Mersey is to my right as I continue south towards The Mersey Tunnel, my route on to The Wirral. It's easy to get confused here and find yourself in the wrong lane, much to the consternation of those short-tempered others, but the confused VW seems unperturbed as it finally chugs its way underground.

The Wirral is basically a peninsula that sticks out from the mainland, as presumably all peninsulas do, silly me. It's 15 miles long and 7 miles wide and the drive around its coastline is just under 40 miles. It has the Irish Sea on top, The River Mersey on its right-hand side and to its left is The River Dee, a natural water border that separates The Wirral from Wales. It has always boasted a strong folk music scene through the years and so my visits there have been plentiful, from the folk festival to The Albion, New Brighton and Birkenhead. There was also a club up in Hoylake for a short time so, yes, I know the area well.

It really is a trip down memory lane today but I have little time to stop and stare, to nick a few choice words from William Wordsworth, as I clock up more miles before bedtime. I drive all the way around The Wirral before it's time to get onto the A540 and follow the signs to Queensferry where we will turn sharp right and join the A548, hopefully finding a quiet backwater to rest up and sleep off the journey. So very soon it will be time to say goodbye to England for a while and enjoy the beautiful countryside of North Wales in the morning. Ah yes, North Wales, the destination of so many holidays as a child. More castles I presume as we are about to enter another country that got pissed off with invasions by the English armies.

I have to say I sense this will be the least pleasurable of all my sleepovers on my whole journey around Britain. I seem to be stuck in a built-up area for the first time and I can't find my way out of. I've managed to find a driveway to a rugby ground so I doubt I'll be disturbed. It isn't ideal by any means and not a patch on some of my overnight stops but at least I'm not overlooked and it offers the bonus of a Chinese takeaway just down the road, so at least I will dine well tonight. There are so many Liverpool gigs juggling around in my head as I tuck into my last supper before leaving England for the second time on my trip. It will never go down in history as the most notorious Last Supper but I'll enjoy my food anyway.

Day 31

Today I prepare myself for road-signs I don't really understand as we head for the uppermost coastline of North Wales.

I must admit I'm not too sure where the border between England and Wales is on this road, but I'm heading for Anglesey today and that's definitely in Wales, an island hanging off the mainland for grim death but a part of Wales just the same. I reckon about a 60-mile journey, and then I'll drive all around the coastline of the island and get back to the mainland over The Menai Bridge before close of the day.

The trip around the island is around 130 miles and so driving around it will push my average miles per day up a bit. To head towards the island I reach Prestatyn, I know that's in Wales too, in the county of Denbighshire. I can't remember having been to Prestatyn before, but it seems to be an interesting place so I look forward to having a quick look round as a quick break from driving along beside the sea.

Well, here we are, and what a delightful beach where The Irish Sea mildly splashes in to say hello before departing on the evening tide. Looking at the tourist guide the place seems to have, like many other places I've visited, a substantial number of Roman connections, particularly a baths, something they were good at, and a wooden castle that rotted long ago, such a shame The Romans didn't invent creosote.

It doesn't take too long to drive through the town, not particularly interesting after all, and the coastal road to Rhyl has really spectacular views. I remember Rhyl from a tumbleweed gig I did there years ago. The St Johns Ambulance people on hand were treating the audience for loneliness. Would I be wrong in suggesting that Rhyl is the Skegness of North Wales? I'm not too sure but there seems to be an awful lot of caravans dotted around and a few holiday camps too so I'm probably right. I choose not to hang around too long because echoes of that empty gig keep ringing in my ears and it's best forgotten, so I hastily drive the 12 miles to Colwyn Bay, another seaside resort on The Irish Sea. Thankfully I never even tried to sell tickets to a concert here so I feel far more relaxed.

Through I drive and my next stop off is in Llandudno, on a peninsula, like an infant Wirral, so it's basically an in and out job after waving to The Cymru Theatre on the North Shore Beach where I thankfully played a couple of times to more people than I did in Rhyl. Round the tiny peninsula I go and onward to a very special landmark, The Menai Bridge, the glorious, spectacular Menai Bridge.

Having studied Modern British History at college, particularly The Industrial Revolution, I have three heroes, James Brindley who built canals, Isambard Kingdom Brunel who contributed much to engineering with a cigar firmly in his mouth, and Thomas Telford, the incredible man who built The Menai Bridge. I am now in my element as the big white symbol of greatness appears in the distance. Due to my college days I don't need to check anything out as it was all part of my exam revision.

The bridge was completed in 1826. Basically, it stretches across from the Welsh mainland to the island of Anglesey and was much needed as The Menai Straits is a dangerous, greedy water that boasts four tides a day and numerous casualties because of it. Thank God I revised for my exams. So what do

117

you want to know about the bridge that was in my syllabus? Well, it took 7 years to build and the road across the bridge was only 24 feet wide originally and so it had to be widened in later years when horses and carts reached their sell-by dates. In 1826 the journey from London to Holyhead took 36 hours, but with the building of the bridge the travelling time was cut by 9 hours, a quarter, and Thomas became a national hero, particularly with weary Londoners it would seem.

As I cross the mighty bridge, all 1,300 feet of it, I see the plaque bearing a credit to the great man and quite rightly so. How builders and engineers erected such things a few hundred years ago without the modern machinery we have today is beyond us all, but they did and these historic monuments remain in far better condition than our motorways today that seem to crack and fall apart with amazing regularity, especially at night it would seem.

By late afternoon I'm driving the 130 miles around the island, ignoring that railway station with the stupidly long name before returning to The Menai Bridge in the opposite direction. To me it's a statue of ingenuity and I take my hat off to Thomas Telford, a Scottish hero.

The one and only show I ever did on Anglesey was at The RAF Valley airbase at Holyhead, just after The Falklands War, so I suppose there needs to be another war if I'm ever to appear there again. In my ignorance I don't even know if there is a theatre on Anglesey. RAF Valley is a flying training base these days so I assume the demographic would be considerably younger that those I performed to after The Falklands. Blimey, most of a modern-day audience here wouldn't have even been born when that war took place, so no I can't really see me ever performing there again as I would sound more like a history teacher than a musician.

Day 32

Today I take the A487 down to Caernarfon, 130 miles away. It's a stunning drive with The Menai Straits on my right shoulder and ragged, rocky land to my left. The extra miles I'm putting in now will mean I will have reached the shores of Caernarfon Bay by the time it's dark. I only ever came this way once before in my life when my dad took the family on a day trip to Caernarfon Castle. I wasn't into history back then and I would have preferred to play on the beach, sticking Welsh flags in sandcastles. Now I'm fascinated. From the 5th Century Romans onwards there have been more fights here than in all of our school playgrounds put together, including William The Conqueror turning up yet again. According to the castle brochure the building of the castle was never completed. And we think plumbers are a pain. They had a thousand years to sort the place out but hey, builders will be builders.

You may have just noticed I haven't namedropped too many theatres of late. There's a reason for that, the simple fact that not many theatres in North Wales ever booked me. As for Anglesey, my trip yesterday, there was more chance of me becoming a long-distance lorry driver on the Isle of Anglesey than being booked to perform there again, as I explained, but I still enjoyed the drive around it. Why did I never perform too often on the island and its surrounding areas? I think me and the theatres must have come to sort of arrangement whereby I couldn't pronounce many of the towns and many of the towns couldn't pronounce my name so we must have left it at that I suppose. Hey, they booked Tom Jones, an easy name to pronounce, so there must have been some possibility I may well have been right.

South Wales is a different story altogether, but we're not there yet, far from it, and so more theatre mentions will be sparse for a few more days yet. Well, this really has been a long and intensive day so I shall sleep well tonight, a shame really as Wales is the perfect place for counting sheep when you're not too tired. Such a waste.

Day 33

It's a pretty straightforward run down the A499 to Pwllheli but a very special memory awaits me there.

My arrival at Pwllheli will change the pictorial backdrop from Caernarfon Bay to Cardigan Bay, but first things first. Before driving into the town I need to make a diversion into Abersoch otherwise I wouldn't have covered all the coastline here. Abersoch is a kind of cul-de-sac on The Llyn Peninsula so it's another in and out job before I head back into Pwllheli in search of The Gimblet Rock caravan site where I went many times with my mother and father. I'm on that piece of land that, on the map, looks like Britain is holding out its arm as if it's begging, with the two different bays I mentioned above and below. Getting here was a hell of a long journey from East London in my dad's Austin 10. I can't remember how long it took my dad to drive the old Austin 10 from East London up to this area of North Wales but I do recall we used to set off really early in the morning before it was light and get here as darkness began to fall. I suppose there is every chance we travelled at the same speed as I am now doing in the camper van. It was a long journey that made the crusts of our sandwiches go rock hard and our bottles of Ribena reach boiling point. Today isn't such a long journey.

Oh my god, Gimblet Rock Holiday Park is indeed still here and the memories are cascading. Now let me tell you about Gimblet Rock itself. When I was a little boy it was three times taller than Snowdon and I successfully climbed it on my second attempt, getting stuck halfway up on the first. It was one of the first major achievements of my life at that time and here I am again, 65 years later.

There's a delightful coffee shop here where I take in refreshments while I think of those fun days with mum and dad and I have no great desire to rush off in haste. I see little kids running around just like I did back then and it all brings a smile to my face.

Just down the road is Criccieth, yet another town with a castle. In actual fact, it's a well-positioned castle with a beach either side so the war enemy factions could make sandcastles on the beach, just like I did, before going to war and attacking a real castle. It also has a theatre called The Memorial Hall, another which I never ever played, which is just as well as I would have bored the audience rigid for two hours with stories about climbing and nearly falling off Gimblet Rock. There wouldn't have been any time left to sing any songs and I would have woken them up anyway.

For fear of boring you too I'm well-aware I've been hanging around this area too long, wallowing in self-indulgence and so it's time to move on.

Around the bay I drive to Harlech and yes, you've guessed, another castle. I did mention earlier there are over 2,000 castles in Scotland. So how many are there in the whole of Britain? Double that number to 4,000 and you won't be far wrong. It makes you realise what an intolerant, blood-thirsty bunch our ancestors were doesn't it? Before this journey I would have guessed at around 500 and I would have been hopelessly wrong. As I mentioned, when I wrote songs for Bill Bryson's audio book, as we peer at the castles today it's an unanswerable question as to why none of them seemed to have windows, or a roof for that matter. Of course, it's a case of the builders not turning up again.

I know the song Men of Harlech because I heard it sung by Ivor Emmanuel in the Zulu movie as the enemy approached but upon arriving here I have noticed there are women and children of Harlech too.

Back on the open road now, 11 miles south to Barmouth and just across the estuary we reach Dolgellau, a small town where I have strangely appeared in concert a few times during recent times, including at The Royal Ship Hotel, in the tiny market square, and at the 9-hole golf club where they had a music night to raise some much-needed funds. Swinging around from the heights of Dolgellau the white Barmouth Bridge that carries the Barmouth Railway across the estuary, looks splendid, and surprisingly long in comparison to such a small place.

Not too many miles covered today so it's full steam ahead to Aberystwyth, a much bigger place with a university that my eldest daughter attended. I've covered exactly 150 miles since I set out this morning and it's been a pleasant coastal drive beside the channel between North Wales and The Irish Republic. The theatre in Aberystwyth is right on the seafront, basically driving through the town and turning right along The North Beach. I played there once a year for many years until it closed for refurbishment and then all went quiet. I used to love the drive to this particular theatre and it was a real joy to re-live that journey today. Driving home in darkness wasn't quite as exciting as I seem to recall but seeing the amazing Welsh countryside on the way to the gig was something very special. A beautiful part of Britain helped by the fact I achieved a few sell-out concerts here, the reason I didn't return here the same sense of embarrassment within me as I did in Rhyl.

The trembling VW camper van just asked me if we would be driving up Snowdon. It sighed a sigh of relief when I told it we had left Snowdon far behind a few days ago and so there was no need for it to worry.

Back in the 1970s there was a strong university gig circuit for acoustic musicians, until the punk movement killed it stone dead, and a tour of such venues in Wales wasn't that difficult to put together. There was Aberystwyth, Bangor, along with numerous gigs in Cardiff, Newport and Swansea, places I would be visiting shortly as I ventured down from North to South Wales. More and more venues were entering my head as I prepared myself for the drive to more familiar places I visited with more regularity.

This drive around Britain has made me realise why some areas just didn't work for me as a box-office attraction. Sure, I always did really well in Cardiff and Swansea, I still do with lots of people and lots of fun had by all, but some of these other places probably didn't get my songs and stories of London, a city so distant from their own lifestyles. They probably weren't that interested and I sense their reticence to take it all in was a protest against England's capital city rather than anything personal against me. They didn't know me so it couldn't possibly have been personal. This trip has made me see the light after so many years of trying to find answers. As for as me and them are concerned there never were any answers to find. I simply didn't appeal and now I understand. Let me tell you, if this trip gave nothing else but closure here in mid-Wales then I'm pleased I went for it.

Having just read that last paragraph or two I seem to be holding some kind of post-mortem regarding this part of Britain, beating myself a bit maybe, but that isn't my intention at all. To be honest I don't think either party are going to lose sleep, and thinking of losing sleep, I have no intention of doing such a thing tonight. I will continue my journey through Wales tomorrow, to an area I visited often during my earlier days on the British folk scene, yes the British folk scene because I'm in Wales where they sang folksongs in their own language, plucked Welsh harps and yet still found time to listen to my material, for which I'm thankful, now I've come to realise it. See you in the morning.

Day 34

Today I'm heading for St Bride's Bay, situated in the outer region of Pembrokeshire, involving a most welcoming and beautiful drive through The Pembrokeshire Coast National Park. To get there from Aberystwyth I make my way around Cardigan Bay to Aberaeron, a small, highly impressive cluster of brightly painted houses perched above the harbour. It looks like someone has lifted the lid of an artist's box of paints and picked out all the vibrant colours. I'd seen photos of it before but it's far more spectacular to be here and stare at the real thing. Blimey, I wish I owned the DIY shop here, I'd make a fortune.

Down to Fishguard now where the River Gwaun empties out into the bay, punching well above its weight. This little former herring fishing village really does have a history to be proud of. I played at a one-day folk festival here in the late 1960s as a member of a duo called Pisces but I don't mean for one minute that's the part of history the village is proud of.

The Battle of Fishguard in 1797 only lasted two days, one day longer than that festival, but it goes down in history as the last invasion by enemies on British soil when 1,400 French soldiers landed and tried to take over the place without success. How about that for interesting history? Two days? I reckon some of the soldiers must have turned up too late to get their weapons out. They signed the surrender on the site of The Royal Oak pub apparently, quite possibly over a tankard of mead and a packet of cheese and onion crisps. All I remember about the festival when I performed was drinking too much Brains Beer but I probably had some crisps too.

The final part of the 83-mile drive along Cardigan Bay towards the southern end of The Irish Sea sees me arrive in St David's via Aberedby, and it's very windy here, hardly surprising jutting out from the mainland as it does. It's one of the most interesting stop-offs of the whole journey as it's the smallest city in Britain for a tiny population of just a couple of thousand. It boasts a cathedral, just like other cities of course, although it lost city status in 1886, only to be given it back in 1994 with an apology. St David's Cathedral was built by The Normans, the big square tower being the give-away here. St David as we all know is the patron saint of Wales and so this is an area of great importance to the Welsh, even if inhabitants are sparse. I don't really know how they wangled city status, being so tiny, but wangle it they did. The same could be said for Ely in Cambridgeshire.

Looking out to sea I spot Ramsey Island in the distance. It isn't part of the journey as the VW can't make it over there, but it's only 2 miles wide so it doesn't make an awful lot of difference to my final mileage total when I get back to Southampton.

The strange thing is that, despite its small size, Ramsey Island is the 4th largest island in Wales after Anglesey, Holy Island and Skomer. In that respect Wales is nothing like Scotland with its multitude upon multitude of rocky hangers-on of huger proportions as I discovered last week. Compared to that lot Ramsay Island is nothing more than a molehill protruding from the water.

Once again, time and tide wait for no man and so it's time to drop down to Pembroke, site of yet another castle, in the grounds of which I performed at The Pembroke Folk

Festival, organised by Haverfordwest Folk Club, with a band called The Arizona Smoke Review if I remember correctly. It's a far more sheltered part of the Pembroke peninsula, it being on the south side, and I recall more fond memories as I look up to the top of the hill where the gig took place around 40 years ago. I'd hate to do that climb now, but I was younger then.

To get here I had to pass through the oil tanker carpark of Milford Haven and its theatre, The Torch, that I played more times than any other Welsh theatre. Just down the road from the theatre is The Lord Nelson pub/hotel where Horatio himself stayed over one night and had his wicked way with Lady Hamilton by all accounts. It's strange how these stories abound when it was supposed to be a secret affair. Before you ask, no he didn't come to one of my Torch concerts before they went to bed.

Nelson was guest of honour there in 1802, a very much in demand after-dinner speaker after his victory at The Battle of The Nile in 1798. In much demand he set about a British tour, just like me, in the years that followed. The Battle of the Nile afforded him incredible celebrity status although there is no mention as to how many crocodiles he killed in the fight. Maybe I got that wrong. Anyway, I bet his fee went up even higher after winning The Battle of Waterloo three years later when he turned his attentions from crocodiles to railway stationmasters.

I've spent so many days in this area over the years and it's been great to return today and re-visit some of my old musical haunts, but now's the time to down a few pints at The Lord Nelson, raise a glass to the naughty admiral, bottoms up and all that, and get my head down before continuing my

129

journey. It's been the most pleasant of days, full of great memories, but I must move on in the morning.

I recall a comedy folksong that contained the words 'not tonight Josephine, I've just had my Ovaltine,' and I feel just as tired as he did that night. I can't believe I'm closing my eyes where Nelson closed his singular.

Day 35

A quick wash, I trust Nelson and Lady Hamilton did the same before they left here, and now I'm off on the road to Swansea.

My first performance here was at the college folk club in The Adelphi Hotel and I'm curious to see if the place still stands. It's only a short drive of 60 miles from Pembroke to Swansea but the traffic today is horrendous, bumper to bumper, and it seems to be taking forever. Hugging the coastline here is a major chore as roads twist and turn, one minute by the coast and then veering inland. but I had to visit The Mumbles before turning left and making my way into the big city situated on Swansea Bay, quite fittingly I feel, just like Aberdeen Bay you may well remember.

I've never been to The Mumbles before, but it's something that has to be done as I have always been a great admirer of author and poet Dylan Thomas and so I want to pay my respect, to soak up what the creative man soaked up when he was here, beyond booze and cigarettes of course, and it certainly is quite breath-taking. I read his biography and this spot was his escape from the self-inflicted, troubled world in which he lived.

Swansea has grown beyond recognition since I first came here, hardly surprising as I'm talking over 50 years ago, so the same can be said for just about everywhere. I remember I could simply drive along the bay from one end to the other without too much difficulty, find my regulation fish and chip shop, park outside the pub for the evening and do my gig. Err, I don't think so anymore.

Damn, I can't find the Adelphi Hotel in Wind Street and neither can I find my way out of here. I see numerous signs for the M4 motorway but I don't want to go on the bloody M4 motorway because I hate it. How did The Romans make such a good job and roadbuilders have all messed up the art ever since? Mind you, what would they do with all those roadworks if there weren't any motorways to store them on? Maybe it's down to concentration on the job. I doubt if The Romans spent half the day messing about on their mobile phones. In a sadistic kind of way I'm enjoying the challenge of finding the smaller roads that take me further around Swansea Bay to Port Talbot. It can be done. It definitely can be done and I'm going to do it.

Ah, thank heavens, I've just found the B4489. Once again, it's not a particularly long journey from Swansea to Port Talbot, 15 miles at the most, but I want to find a place, somewhere quiet and peaceful, to park up for the night before I hit the industrial spread of Port Talbot. It's difficult to find such a place in this area but I've managed to find a carpark for a recreation park and no-one else is around since it has become dark so this will have to do me.

I didn't quite know what to expect today. The people around here are so friendly, always have been, and attentive audience members that hang on your every word. They love their traditional music and they know their traditional music well. My first tour when I first turned professional was to this very area and, during the late 1960s and 70s there was an abundance of folk clubs in the area from here up into the Welsh valleys, taking in Merthyr Tydfil, Aberdare, Mountain Ash, Bridgend, Barry Island and other places I'm sure that I may have misplaced somewhere in my head. I'll be telling you more about them when I reach Cardiff and my brain starts to dig out more memories of those valley clubs as they were known.

Reading back through these pages it seems I have a fixation for fish and chip shops, but that isn't quite true. When I first went on the road I didn't have much choice. There were no fast-food outlets and petrol stations sold nothing but petrol. I took up stamp collecting at the time, not the Penny Blacks as you'd expect but more Green Shield Stamps which were responsible for the numerous Pyrex dishes I accumulated. One tour could easily fill up a whole book of the things. They were one of my earliest perks of being a professional musician. It was either fish and chips, pie and chips, or just chips if I was short of funds. The only other option was to starve. There were no takeaways after a gig, they hadn't even been invented, so social events after a folk club were back to people's houses for cheese and biscuits and copious amounts of home-made wine.

Day 36

Four weeks on the road completed and I'm loving every minute of it.

I've played in Port Talbot a good few many times over the years and followed their industrial plight in recent times on the TV news. The steelworks were its lifeblood for a hundred years or more, creating jobs and a tight-knit community, but things have changed so much in the modern world and there is now so much unemployment around here. Maybe because it's raining today, but the whole area looks a little on the bleak and defeated side.

Such a downturn is a huge industry such as steel obviously affects the music industry too. When people lose their jobs they're not in a position to come to gigs and so the affect snowballs and everyone suffers. Folk Clubs were always small venues and admission wasn't much, bearing in mind most of the audience were students, but now such clubs are as scarce as money in places like Port Talbot and this part of the trip has made me realise there's always people worse off than you. How I miss those vibrant days on the folk scene when money meant nothing because none of us had any. The only folky gig in Port Talbot was in the working men's club and they would never book a singer who was playing somewhere else in Wales that week. They demanded exclusivity, a difficult thing when it was so far from home, so they never constituted a tour date.

There used to be a folk club organiser called Dublin Moran who used to organise mini tours around the area South Wales but, as I say, times have changed and the British folk club scene has now dwindled down dismally to a trickle since the bad times of 2020 and 2021, nowhere more so than around here. Yes, it really does make me sad to think of the great times that used to be here for me to enjoy, drinking Brains Beer or that home-made wine until I couldn't take any more and singing way into the night in the house or flat of someone who had put me up for the night. Hey, at least I did it and I have the great memories to prove it as I drive through Port Talbot and out the other side, down through Pyle and onwards towards Porthcawl at the bottom of the bay. We're 19 miles on now in Mid-Glamorgan.

As you have already read I went to North Wales on a few holiday excursions as a kid, but never South Wales, and yet, according to the tourist guide here, Porthcawl has no less than 7 beaches, one for each dwarf. Maybe dad should have driven us here as it wouldn't have been such a long journey from East Ham. Ha-ha, after all these years I have now realised my dad didn't know everything after all.

I park up at Trecco Bay Beach and admire the view. It's cold today but still some brave souls have covered themselves in rubber and are floating about in the sea on lumps of wood until they fall off in an ungainly way.

Porthcawl overlooks The Bristol Channel, as a reminder to me that I'm not far from being back in England. Now then, what can I say about Porthcawl? This is the home of The Porthcawl Male Voice Choir, one of many such ensembles in Wales and they're a highly respected bunch of vocalists by all accounts who delight in always having a celebrity guest to join them. I only mention them because I have no personal musical connection to this place whatsoever, but with music being such an important part of both my life and this journey it would be remiss of me not to give my passion a mention whilst here in Porthcawl, albeit a bit odd and far away from my own style of music, I admit.

What else can I say? I decide to spend the day exploring all of those 7 beaches if I possibly can as there are no venues to re-visit. Coney Beach is where a fairground can be found but I have no desire to add a goldfish to the journey. To the west is Rest Bay and to the east is Newton Beach. It's all sandy and nice to stroll along until I get slightly more adventurous and try rock hopping on Pink Bay beach.

I end up at Seafront Beach, three out of seven wasn't bad, so named for obvious reasons and I climb back into the camper van after taking on supplies from the local Co-op.

If I'm brutally honest, I'm none the wiser, a beach is a beach and sand is sand. I may have even got the names of the beaches wrong but it doesn't matter, I'm not a geography teacher, but my short stay here reminded me of the fact that there are more stars in The Universe than grains of sand on Planet Earth. Just think about that for a moment. It's an amazing fact but I'd like to know who counted the bloody things and how long did it take them?

It's almost time to leave Porthcawl as I try to work out a place where I can sleep before attacking Cardiff in the morning. I'm sorry I couldn't make this section more interesting. I tried but I failed. I do like the sound of Newton Village as I drive through. I doubt very much if the great man of the same name ever lived here but I shall keep one eye open for falling apples just in case. Tomorrow I just happen to know my head will be full of music venues where I have performed over the years so it will be a self-indulgent day, but hey, you're more than welcome to join me and come along on the continuous nostalgic trip down memory lane. Goodnight.

Day 37

I'm excited this morning, but I'm wary too. I don't think my VW camper van is going to enjoy the hustle and bustle of Cardiff too much, but it has to be done. Before we head off, I top him up with oil as a bit of a treat, a bit of a softener. All will be fine.

It would normally be a 30-mile trip to Cardiff along the M4 but not for me as I'm taking the coast route, taking in Bridgend and dropping down to Barry before swinging round into Cardiff. 47 miles later I'm on the outskirts of the big city and I need to find a way through the maze that keeps me beside the water's edge. The A4232 helps considerably.

Cardiff Bay has played a major part in the transformation of this area in recent years. It used to be where coal clinker boats would load up before heading off around the world, but it's all changed now as it's become a hub of things to do and a new centre for the film and TV industries. I first came to this rejuvenated part of Cardiff to work with a cartoon company called Siriol, but my links with Cardiff go much further back than that.

As I mentioned yesterday the Valleys tour really was something special. The folk scene has always been the skint member of the music industry and many folk clubs sprung up in skint areas during the late 1960s and early 1970s. None more so than here. I am itching to make the trip today but to go inland would be against the rules I made myself and it would be unfair to other inland venues I would love to have visited on my coastal journey around Britain, so I can do nothing more than describe it to you.

The Welsh Valley Tour always began in Merthyr Tydfil, 24 miles north of Cardiff, with a lunchtime gig at The Hoover factory, before heading down to The Railway Hotel, Aberdare, paying respects to the young victims of The Aberfan Disaster as I passed the gravestones up on the hill. Then we played Mountain Ash, Port Talbot and Bridgend folk clubs before the more lucrative Cardiff gigs, namely The Locomotive and The Marchioness of Bute folk club in Frederick Street. An even better pay-day occurred with a booking at what was then Llandaff College, a subsidised music gig and a god send to boot. Newport folk club we played on the way back home. There was no M4 in those days and so the Newport gig was always followed for a very long drive. Mind you, we still drank loads after the gig as this was long before breathalysers. We only blew into bags when our chips were too hot. It's the very same Newport I will head for shortly, once I have done the rounds of theatres related to my past. It's so strange, there are so many in Cardiff I find it difficult to single them out, but still I try.

The easiest is St David's Hall, the big boy, where I supported Welshman Tom Jones for a few nights. In my own right I played The New Theatre and a place I seem to recall as The Royal College of Speech and Drama, but I may have got that one slightly wrong.

In more recent times I have performed a few times at The Acapela Theatre, built within what looks like an old church with a state-of-the-art recording studio upstairs. They make their own pizzas in giant ovens before the gig and the smell in the air is to die for.

Oh yes, so many venues, but none of them are on our agenda today as we head off east out of Cardiff, towards the aforementioned Newport, a place that has suffered the same, sad, steel decline as Port Talbot. There is green grass and countryside between Cardiff and Newport and I intend to find it to make the journey more enjoyable and to find a place for an overnight. The journey from Cardiff to Newport is only 15 miles on a straight road but we all know I'm having none of that. Time to go exploring along the coastline beneath the awful M4 motorway.

We travel beside The Bristol Channel with Portishead in full view on the other side and Weston Super Mare to its right, further down towards the open sea. This part of the journey is proving a challenge as there are far more mudbanks around than roads, but by fair mains and foul, we make it to Newport. Every year to this day I perform in Llanhennock Village Hall for a friend of mine who makes Welsh harps so I know the area well.

Although their football team is called Newport County, Newport is a city, smaller than Cardiff and bigger than St David's. The River Usk passes through and the B4237 takes me to The Riverfront Theatre, the venue of my last concert in Newport. I seem to remember an ancient shipwreck of some sort sticking out of the water here the last time but I can't seem to find it this time. On the history front, Newport has a castle that the good old Normans built. It makes you wonder what else The Normans did other than build castles and churches. They couldn't have all been builders, surely not. Surely must have been bus or train drivers.

I leave Newport on the A449 to Carleon and Llantrisant but after just a couple of miles I've taken a smaller road to Caldicot and I'm back on the coast. It isn't long before The Severn Bridge is in sight, but, once again, I have to avoid it and drive on to Chepstow before heading back to the area I see on the other side of The Bristol Channel. The Bristol Channel is actually The River Severn and some know it as The Severn Estuary. I know it more as a wide strip of inconvenient water and it should therefore be filled in, just like people do with unwanted garden ponds. I rest my case.

It's quite a diversion, avoiding the bridge, so I decide to negotiate my way through Chepstow and spend the night on the edge of The Forest of Dean in Lydney in Gloucestershire. I never saw a 'welcome to England' sign like I did when I left Scotland, but anyway, I'm now well and truly back in England. I drive through Newerne Street and there doesn't seem to be much more than that to the place, so it's time to get out and explore. I always find church parish noticeboards are a gem for information. They're also handy if you're looking for a second-hand pram or dog-sitters.

There used to be an Iron Age fort here, made of wood I hasten to add, before The Romans came and built a temple on top of it, careless boys. This tiny place I've never been to before, indeed I'd never even heard of the place, can boast a history that very few other small villages can boast, and it's a boast that ties in rather nicely with my musical themes throughout this journey. Can you believe The Beatles, yes The Beatles, played Lydney Town Hall on August 31st, 1962, and they went down so well the committee promised to book them back. It's been a Hard Day's Night so I'm camping up here for the night because I don't want to leave this unknown musical shrine right now. Everything can wait while I take in this amazing fact.

I stare at the somewhat inobtrusive Lydney Town Hall and imagine what it must have been like that night way back in 1962. It's strange considering we visited Liverpool a week or so ago and yet I feel closer to The Beatles here than I did back in the land of Penny Lane and Strawberry Fields. Sitting here I feel I could almost reach out and touch them. It's a tiny venue and they must have run up this little road to escape the screaming fans. Oh my god, this is musical history in the extreme, and it's in a little place I'd never heard of until today. I feel the whole trip was almost worth it just for this unexpected experience. I just love it. Oh yes, the number times I ran down roads to escape screaming fans. The answer you're looking for is zero.

There are so many Beatles songs ringing in my ears right now. Yesterday, Liverpool seemed so far away. Now I'm even further down the long and winding road. Goodnight.

Day 38

Wow, wasn't that a surprise? It certainly was, but now I need to continue on that long and winding road to quote one of the Fab Four if you didn't get the play on words the first time. I'm heading very eastward at the moment and I need to get to a point where I can cross The River Severn and go back west, young man. I drive through Cinderford in search of such a bridge. My plan is to drive until I'm back to The Severn Bridge on the south side of the river after driving through Thornbury. I love bridges, just as well I suppose, and I happen to know there's a Services in the shadows of the bridge and it's worth taking the time to find out more about The Severn Bridge that I have crossed so many times during my career. I'm quite happy to spend a few quid and pay my carparking fee to enjoy a few hours taking in the splendour of such a construction.

So, basically, this suspension bridge reaches from Monmouthshire in Wales, where we were yesterday, to Gloucestershire, where we are today. My hero who I have introduced you to before, Thomas Telford, had the idea for the bridge back in 1824, but nothing much happened apart from the building of a railway bridge to speed up the post. Before then, the only route across was by ferry.

The bridge we see today wasn't opened until 1966 and it has to be said it's one hell of an engineering achievement, not dissimilar to the Forth Bridge we saw up in Scotland.

I fully understand that this may be boring to some, but I consider anything to do with British history a bit of a gem and anything involving Thomas Telford a gold nugget. It's amazing to think he started working on the idea 140 years before it was built. I suppose the same could be said for Charles Babbage who came up with the idea of a computer in 1792. These boys were clever in the extreme and I take my hat off to them once again, just like I did to Brunel and Brindley earlier on this journey. If nothing else Babbage had a song written about which has always gone down well.

Anyway it's a short day in terms of mileage as I indulge in my own history lesson but tomorrow I promise to make up for lost time as we head west.

Day 39

As I drive along with the Bristol Channel on our right I look across to the South Wales coastline that I negotiated in its entirety just a few days ago. It feels special, as if it belonged to me for a short time, which of course it didn't and now the realisation is it belongs to Wales and I'm back in England. I wouldn't say this is the most picturesque part of the expedition, but it has to be done as I make my way down to the West Country. I resented paying carparking fees, the first of the entire trip, but that had to be done too to soak up my experiences regarding The Severn Bridge.

I had a nice shower in the Services this morning, a true luxury. and I feel well and truly up for a fair day's driving as promised. The plan today is to reach the seaside town of Weston Super Mare, home of one of my favourite theatres, The Playhouse. However, to get there is a game of backwards and forwards as we weave in and out of areas that don't even have a road, let alone a remote route along the coast. With such haphazard navigation I sense we will be travelling much further than the 25 miles I'd reckoned when I planned the route before I left Southampton. The places to drive in and out of are Avonmouth, Portishead, Clevedon, Nailsea and finally Weston Super Mare.

You may well notice I've given Bristol a miss, despite its size and history. It's due to an engrained issue I have with the place. Yes, I played the once named Colston Hall numerous times, but when my life began on the road over fifty years ago I couldn't get a booking in a Bristol folk club for love nor money. It was always very much a closed scene that didn't welcome intruders from London. For that reason brought about all those years ago I have never been there and I know very little about the place other than The Clifton Suspension Bridge is a bit special. It seems ridiculous to me that I can only attribute 3 of my 3,000 concerts during my career to this massive city. In the last 20 years I've only been to Bristol once and that was to pick someone up at the airport. Even more ridiculous is that my daughter, Rosie, lives close to Bristol but we've never driven into the place for a drink or a meal.

As I proceed into North Somerset I now sense the West Country is looming ever closer. I've never been too sure where the West Country begins. Living in Salisbury I like to think I live on its boundary because I love the West Country so much and therefore pretend I'm a West Country resident when I'm not really. On this particular part of the journey I'm placing Weston Super Mare into that box and I look forward to arriving there later today. Or so I thought.

Well, it had to happen I suppose, a flat tyre. There's no way I can complain about the camper van's performance as VW has done such a wonderful job, but today the poor old thing isn't feeling at all well. Its sudden illness has created a first on the journey as I switch on my redundant mobile phone to get someone out to help with the repair. Some VWs have their spare wheels bolted to the front beneath the windscreen, like some kind of bulbous nose, but VW was designed differently and I need assistance.

The wait for help seems endless and I feel so helpless, Sadly I'm completely useless at anything mechanical and can do very little other than sit by the roadside and make myself a cup of coffee on the primus stove. As I sit here I wonder how many passing motorists are pondering on why an idiot like me would sit here drinking coffee when there are so many far more desirable places to stop and have a quiet break. If only they knew I agree with them entirely, but like it or not I have a feeling I'm stuck here for the day what with waiting for roadside assistance and then finding a new tyre that will fit an old VW and getting it fitted on. Damn.

Day 40

So, hello the West Country and Weston Super Mare, finally, the town with one of the loveliest theatres and some of the most aggressive traffic wardens ever hatched. The big problem with that is that all roads there have double-yellow lines if they're not offering parking to permit holders only and the road where the stage door is situated is no exception. There's no solution to the problem so every time you play The Playhouse you have to include a parking ticket in your expenses. I drive past the theatre just for old time's sake without stopping and for the first time there isn't a traffic warden in sight. Sod's Law I think they call that. If I choose to unload and park legally it would be a good quarter of an hour walk back to the theatre. The staff are the friendliest you could find but their hands are tied by power-crazed traffic wardens who know performers have to park to unload their gear, meaning that they lay in wait when people like me arrive. What I don't get is that the town relies on tourists and holidaymakers and of course entertainment is a major part of a holiday or a casual break, but the council have done nothing to make our job easier. Come on Weston, you have an amazing theatre at The Playhouse so get a grip.

Did you know The Bristol Channel has the second highest tidal rise in the whole world? That fact is a huge hazard for any swimmer who dares to splash around there, but there are some superheroes who have actually swum across to Wales. Kathleen Thomas was the first to do so successfully in 1927 when she made it across from Weston to Penarth in 7 hours 20 minutes. For those brave souls who try, it can be double the 11 miles across due to various tides that rear up like fences at The Grand National. Knowing my luck I'd probably get a parking ticket waiting for the tide to come in.

As promised I'm making up the miles today so it's farewell to my friends in Weston Super Mare and Somerset too as I head on to the A361 towards Ilfracombe in North Devon after stopping for a cup of tea a cake in Lynton. For those of you who have driven on this road you can imagine how VW camper van quaked in his tyres when he saw the gradient of the hill that took us there. It's more like a ski-slope than a road. The fact I am now in the West Country is now well beyond doubt.

On the way I made a diversion into Minehead, the right thing to do as a mark of musical respect as Status Quo started out at Butlins in Minehead and became one the most resilient rock bands in the history of music. It had to be done and it only added half an hour to my journey.

As I travelled through I was able to touch Exmoor National Park and the beautiful villages of Dunster, Brendon and Porlock. I'd love to slip further inland as I love Exmoor so much, but once again it isn't allowed.

I suggest the dressing room of The Landmark Theatre in Ilfracombe boasts the most spectacular views from any dressing room window in Britain. I love to go and sit on the sea wall on the other side of the stage door entrance when my soundcheck is complete and watch the sea attack the rocks below. There's a tiny horseshoe-shaped beach to the right and some sort of monument on top of a high cliff further to the right but I've always found an excuse not to bother to climb up and have a closer look

I remember well when The Landmark Theatre was opened and everyone commented on the two-pointed domes that protruded from its roof that resembled a bra Madonna wore on a world tour at the time. The place is still known today as Madonna's Bra. It took the place of The Pavilion Theatre that suffered from a fire and we did shows there on a stage with nothing at the back other than a black curtain and a tarpaulin to keep out the weather. As they always say, the show had to go on and go on it did. The Landmark hit hard financial times a few years ago but I had to take possibly a last look at a lovely theatre with a dressing room door carved into the side of a cliff. Unique it most certainly is.

. There's another theatre here worthy of mention too, The Gaiety Theatre, once managed by the parents of Peter Sellers who was obviously an Ilfracombe resident.

Here's an interesting fact, Alice Phillips, who lived at 85 High Street, Ilfracombe, an amateur actress who supported the arts of the town is noted as a Titanic survivor in 1912 when she climbed aboard lifeboat number 12. Her father, Escott Phillips, also of the same address in Ilfracombe, sadly never made it to a lifeboat and was officially lost at sea.

My time in Ilfracombe is now done and it's time to head uphill and out of town in a southerly direction towards Woolacombe. It's been a while since I've driven along beside The Atlantic Ocean but here it is once again. It's so odd to think that it splashes the coastline of our island at its northern-most and southern-most extremities and I've taken in both on this journey. Interestingly, Woolacombe also marks the spot where The Bristol Channel finally disappears into The Atlantic.

The beaches along this particular part of our coastline, especially Woolacombe Sands, are just stunning, not as long and straight as those we saw in Suffolk and Norfolk but they are so easy to the eye and it didn't take much persuasion from me to convince myself to spend the night adjacent to the holiday park on the way out of town.

I decided earlier to lock VW and take a stroll along the golden sands, paddling in The Atlantic as a kind of therapy for weary feet that have been working the pedals for well over 3 weeks. The water was freezing cold and yet delightfully refreshing. As I did so I looked back at sorry-looking VW camper van, covered in salt from the numerous days of sea air. It deserved better and so I did the deed when I returned and got the sponge and bucket of water on the go, hoping my mechanical pal found it as equally and delightfully refreshing as I found the sea. I wouldn't say for one moment the old wagon looked showroom standards but at least I'd got rid of the white blotches of salt on its bodywork.

There used to be a music gig at The Old Mill but the problem was that it was so far away I had to get more than one gig to make a profit. Many musicians travelled by train back in the day but it made life so difficult what with carrying a guitar, an overnight bag and a box of albums to sell on the door. I chose to go by car, even if the cost of petrol was somewhat prohibitive. The other gig to make it viable was at The Joiners Arms in Bideford. Then we would travel down to Cornwall just like I'm doing on this journey if we found a few more dates to put in the diary. Two dates were a tour back then because it also included a day travelling down and an extra day to travel back. It's ironic I suppose that I travelled around back then in the early 70s at the same speed as I travel around Britain in 80 days. It all came back to me today as I travelled around my old West Country haunts, the wonderful gigs I did here and I couldn't to get back to Bideford where I loved to hang out with other folksingers. It was a brilliant social scene back then and so many of my old mates from then are no longer around to know I'm undertaking this reincarnation of travel.

Day 41

Me and my sparkling clean VW are heading further down into Devon today but before we get stuck into putting some miles behind us I need to drive past and pay my respects to a tiny venue in Bideford, not The Joiners Arms but The Paladium, spelling correct by the way. It's what I call a sardine theatre and the atmosphere has been incredible every time I've played there in recent years. I was hoping to see the steam train chug along on the other side of the estuary too, but my luck wasn't in.

So, I am now well and truly in glorious Devon, known for its clotted cream and so, of course, I have to indulge. Do you know the difference between a Devon cream tea and a Cornish cream tea? Yes, there is actually a difference. With one you put cream on top of the strawberry jam in a scone one and with the other the cream goes on first. Sadly, although I'm full of irrelevant facts, I have no idea which is which, an admission that will not make me lose any sleep.

I intend to make it to the final Devon outpost of Hartland before nightfall. It's almost on the northern border between Devon and Cornwall and the area is known as The Hartland Peninsula. It's the most west-northerly village in Devon and was once a port in Tudor times. Hartland Abbey is of particular interest as we haven't passed too many abbeys on route as most seemed to be built inland and thus out of bounds to us.

It's a windy day, so much so that VW is wobbling about but I find a small lay-by outside the village where I can take shelter from the weather. I open a tin of pears and cover them with Devon full clotted cream. Some will say it's not too good for the heart but I really don't care. My heart has suffered more shocks than this during my 50 years and more on the road. Transport cafes must have taken their toll on me in some way but I seem to have survived the culinary onslaught of sausage, egg, bacon, baked beans and mushrooms, scooped up with a doorstop slice of white bread and washed down with a sugary mug of tea. Hey, compared to that a bowl of clotted cream is a walk in the park for my heart. I close my eyes with utmost content. Tomorrow I head for Cornwall.

Strange as it may seem, we shall be returning to Devon later in our journey as it is the only English county with two separate coastlines, The Irish Sea in the north as we discovered and the English Channel in the south as we shall see later.

Day 42

Travelling down to the West Country at a weekend is not to be recommended as it's what everyone else seems to have planned to do after leaving work on a Friday afternoon.

During the unfortunate events of 2020 and 2021 Cornwall became the number one place to visit in Britain when flights abroad were cancelled, airports thus had closed and cruise ships had dropped anchor in Weymouth. The idea of a holiday in Cornwall became such a great idea they eventually had to close all the carparks and turn people away as vehicles on the M5 backed up for endless miles, their tempers and radiators overheating.

As the 2021 lockdown eased it seemed as though 59 million of the 60 million people living in Britain were heading in this direction and the whole of the West Country was in danger of sinking into the Atlantic Ocean along with a trillion pasties floating across in the largest ever convoy to The United States of America. That's not how I remember this most tranquil of counties at all and I suppose it will return to such a laid-back place once we all return to some kind of a normality.

Cornwall is where artists, writers and musicians love to congregate, away from the hustle and bustle of city life, yet it seems busier than usual today, certainly busier than I ever remember it to be. Yes of course there are more cars on the roads these days, faster and more reliable cars that make Cornwall more accessible in the modern world but the minor roads of the county were never built for such an invasion.

I've managed to stay off the M5 myself, but others are attempting the same alternative routes too and it's become a bit of a nightmare. Horns are being blasted around here for the first time in years. Horse-drawn carts never had horns and come to think of it neither did horses.

It's a real shame but I sense today will be a complete write-off for me as the holidaymakers, potential holidaymakers more accurately, are blocking my westward journey and I don't want to overheat VW's engine. It doesn't deserve any more injuries now it has recovered from the flat tyre.

Planning anything today will be a complete and utter waste of time so I'll park up and have a day of leisure, just like I did up at Loch Ness. If you really do want to meet a monster, by the way, then meet some of the motorists on the M5 motorway. I promise that you'll be spoilt for choice. I knew weekends would be busy but this is more hectic than I'd anticipated.

Cornwall had a folk scene second to none as the folk revival, as they called it in the late 1960s, gathered pace and became the cool music scene to be part of, especially for hippies and students. This county was one of the few that had seasonal folk clubs, probably due to the weather and the additional fact that enough people lived here to fill the halls. Because of this Cornwall became well organised with any potential bookings considered from late Spring to the end of Autumn. During the winter months club gatherings were small, usually in the rooms of pubs, sitting round an open fire with tankards of ale, singing songs of the past in their own Breton-influenced dialect. It all conjures up a wonderful picture of artistic contentment. It wasn't until the weather changed that singers like me, the professionals if you like, were invited down here and there were ample folk clubs to give us all work.

Suddenly, when the fire wasn't blazing, chairs were placed in lines with a gangway down the middle, concert fashion, and the whole atmosphere changed, not for the bad or for the good, but it just changed. How big were these clubs? A small sing-around venue could be as small as a dozen regulars and a night with a guest at the more successful clubs would have been around 100 or 150. It wasn't a big scene by any means, it never was and it never will be. Young music-lovers filled the rooms but those young music-lovers have grown old and aren't really being replaced by a new generation so the folk scene we know today is eroding away like the cliffs at Lyme Regis. Will it ever recover? Recover from what? It's just the way it is. Music goes in cycles but folk music goes in Zimmer frames, it's a fact of life I'm afraid, but our traditional songs will live on forever. Maybe in 100 years' time they will be singing the songs we write today. That's what the folk scene is all about, re-visiting and re-discovering, just like I am on my journey around Britain in 80 days.

As I ponder these thoughts in The Crown beer-garden I also declare you cannot beat a good ploughman's lunch. Crusty bread and a fair wedge of Cheddar never did anyone any harm other than constipation, but I suppose those old-time workers of the land used to work it off after lunch as they walked the fields behind a weary horse.

As I sit here in the beer-garden I can't help but notice the rust, rich-coloured soil. It's unique to this part of the country due to the granite further down and although it's rich in colour it's relatively infertile. I remind myself that this area was full of mines and quarries through the centuries, an industrial area in its own way, yet complete different to other industrial parts of Britain. I'm also reminded that, once upon a time, the quaint fishing villages I'm visiting weren't considered quaint places built for tourists, but clusters of worker's cottages who relied on the perilous seas to make a living. Unlike holiday resorts abroad Cornwall wasn't built to attract tourists and today the congested narrow roads of the county prove my point. The visitors would have all returned home by the morning, allowing me to continue my journey in a sedate manner.

Day 43

So where are we heading today? Padstow is your answer. But first we must drive into Bude which is a kind of cul-de-sac town as you drive in via a road that doesn't really go anywhere else, so once again it's an in and out job, just like the hokey-cokey, as we have done so many times before at other coastal retreats on this adventure.

To reach Padstow we pass alongside so many stunning places along the way, starting with Crackington Haven, followed by Boscastle and Tintagel. Of course, Tintagel Castle is associated with the legend of King Arthur and the Knights of the Round Table. Also, many years ago the Duke of Cornwall locked his wife in the castle when he went to war with the words 'Won't be long love.' It's perpendicular architecture, stretching up towards the sky, is a compelling sight, as though it seems to be standing there overseeing the safety of the locals as it presumably the Duke's wife in his absence. Oh yes, and it's haunted too. It may be him or it may be her, we shall never know.

The strange thing is, despite it being a such a folksong area, I performed here rarely over the years. Maybe that was right as they still go more for the traditional singer here rather than the more modern songwriter such as me, just like they did around the open fires. Nothing wrong with that, I love our traditional folk music so I have no complaints.

Further along this northern stretch of coast I come to Port Isaac, made famous in recent times by the singing of Fisherman's Friends. They made a film about them and suddenly Port Isaac has become known around the world with tourist-attraction status. Is this ringing a bell? It's reminding me of my trip to Pennan when in Scotland. The Local Hero movie and the Mark Knopfler music? Oh yes, it's ringing a bell alright. Well, here we are again with a similar scenario in Cornwall. It's also the location for the TV series Doc Martin, so it's well exposed on screens both big and small. Not that Port Isaac needed such fame and glory because it's a beautiful place anyway and popular with visitors in its own right.

It used to be a fishing village specialising in the hunting for pilchard shoals but that industry disappeared along with the pilchards and so the place had to rely on its beauty and tourism. Old English backdrops are loved all around the world through period dramas and films adapted from classic books of the past. Britain is a collection of glorious scenery that lends itself to film making. Port Isaac is definitely up there at the top of the league of locations.

What about Cornwall as a county? It once had a thriving tin industry with mines stretching out beneath the sea. It has its own native tongue too, popularised by the singing of Brenda Wootton, and that's quite a unique boast around Britain. The first manuscripts relating to Cornwall in written form go way back to the 1st Century and yet, through all this, it remains one of Britain's most unspoilt counties despite the invasion of visitors that prevented my progress yesterday.

Padstow doesn't have any sea today. It has wandered off to somewhere or other making the walls very high, particularly at this carpark. I thought VW had developed a bit of an exhaust cough but I now realise it may well be vertigo. Put it this way, it's a hell of a drop. This place has its own traditions, particularly on May Day, a fertility celebration and a wish for a successful harvest, sowing seeds in two different ways then. Morris dancers come out to play and a good time is had by all. In Padstow there's the hobby horse, or 'obby 'orse, parade through the town, a tradition that goes back well over 100 years.

Folk clubs abounded in Cornwall and it's like a game of hide and seek to remember the various venues and to in search of them on this trip. I've remembered more down this way than anywhere else in Britain, I just don't know if the pubs still exist. There were clubs in Camelford, Bodmin, here in Padstow and a gig called The Folk Cottage in Mitchell that my memory just took me to, even though I have no idea where Mitchell actually is so there will be no re-visit there.

The only area here, although further inland, where I started in a pub and made it to a theatre is Truro, having played The Swan pub and the slightly bigger, ok much bigger, Theatre for Cornwall. I recall it being a theatre with a strange stage door location in what seemed to be an old cattle or corn market. If I were passing that way I'd check it out but it isn't on my itinerary, so I have to remain confused.

It has to be done before I pack up for the night, so time for an authentic Cornish pastie. Now, where's the brown sauce?

Day 44

I've enjoyed entering Cornwall from a different direction to that which normally brings me here. There won't be so many daily miles undertaken while I drive around down here as there are so many quaint villages, outposts and landmarks to visit, each with memories to conjure up. The roads are narrower too so I'll take things nice and steady.

I need to drive inland a little this morning to negotiate a small estuary, but my ultimate destination is Newquay, which means I have tons of time on my hands as its less than 20 miles although I should clarify that driving 20 miles in Cornwall takes about the same time as travelling 40 in most of the other counties.

Today, I want to give a wave to a venue that housed one of my favourite gigs just before lockdown hit us.

Even with the winding roads and endless stream of caravans and motorhomes, if they're still around after the weekend, it's hardly going to be a taxing day behind the wheel so I'll just take in the beautiful scenery. It's good to give VW an easy day too as it has been as good as gold for the last few weeks and it deserves a gentle run.

I was only thinking this morning how different the various coastlines are around Britain and the example is, let's say, Cornwall and Suffolk. Ok, they're both by the sea but how many fishing villages are there in Cornwall compared to how many in Suffolk? There are definitely more on the west of our island and yet there are far more fish in the waters off our east coast. There's no doubt about it, we are all living on a very confusing lump of land. To prove my point further, how many islands are there off the west coast of Scotland as opposed to those off Lincolnshire? Each area seems to have its own attributes. Additionally, The North Sea is actually on the eastern coastline and The Irish Sea is off Scotland. Look at all the watery inlets off the north of Scotland and compare them to the few hanging around the south of England. You see, the actual physical features on which we live are as varied as us people who live here. A further point of proof is that I couldn't cover as many miles down the left-hand side as I could down the right-hand, due to a lack of straight coast roads and such is the case whilst I am in Cornwall. Today I'm only driving those 20 miles to Newquay and I make no apologies for the lack of miles covered. Hey, I'm in Cornwall and I'm enjoying it.

I played The Lane Theatre, Newquay twice in two years before lockdown came along and many members of the audience told me how grateful they were I'd travelled that far to perform for them. I never understood that. I mean to say, it isn't exactly a million miles away, and I didn't arrive on a sleigh pulled by huskies, but it's obviously too far down for some performers to go if their comments to me were accurate. There's also The Stagecoach Theatre here, by the way, but I've never been there and know nothing about the place but I thought it should be mentioned out of courtesy.

To tell you the truth I don't know much about Newquay itself as the Lane Theatre is on the outskirts and so I've decided to drive in and take the place in for the very first time. I've heard many times it's the surfing centre of England so we can assume it's where The Atlantic Ocean loses its temper and gets angry at Fistral Bay.

Although not in the Stonehenge league there are pre-historic burial mounds in Newquay which only goes to show that surfing can be a very dangerous sport and has been for many, many years. They also found proof of The Bronze Age at Trethellan Farm which, with my logic, means they also buried lots of surfers who didn't win gold or silver but came third. That's about all the tourist guide wants to tell me as there's more adverts than information, but never mind.

After I've driven into Newquay I head back out again and make my way towards a strangely shaped part of Cornwall that looks like a hand with just a thumb and one finger, on which we find Crantock, Holywell Bay and Cubert, three Cornish outposts that have little protection from the weather. I park up in what seems to be a field but there doesn't seem to be anyone around so I'll take the risk.

No, you can't just park up and make a brew like I used to back in the day. Huge concrete carparks didn't exist when I began my career on the road but it's so different nowadays. The countryside seems to be choked up with private land these days and they don't welcome a VW camper van. Even lay-bys have signs that tell me overnight parking is forbidden. Why? Let's not even go there. I suppose it's because local councils make a fair wedge of cash from their designated carparks so they don't want me to just park wherever I feel. It's all a far cry from parking right outside a pub and falling back into the camper after the gig. Sometimes a friendly landlord would place beer-crates in the road to make sure my VIP space wasn't taken by another vehicle. Imagine that happening today, no chance.

I have to say that Scotland was different. I had no problem pitching up for the night up there, but in England it's something I didn't allow for when I planned my journey. Hey, if you owned a VW camper van would you worry about where you could park it overnight? No, I didn't either, but I should have done. I prefer trees to long stretches of concrete and country lanes to giant megastore complexes on the edges of towns, but I didn't realise I edged towards breaking the law by having such green expectations.

Day 45

We've been on this journey now for 5 weeks, you and I, and we've taken in so many beautiful places. I've driven you through some major cities too when I had no choice. I have no particular favourite area as each has brought about a different memory or story and variety, as we all know, is the spice of life.

It's only a short diversion around this odd one-fingered hand I described to you and once finally negotiated, today we drive further south to the artist's haven, St Ives. The distance from Newquay to St Ives is 32 miles, but don't be deceived. Today I take in more tiny coastal villages than on any other day of the journey and I don't want to miss one.

So it is that I find myself on single-track roads that were obviously originally built for a horse and cart as I find each hidden Cornish gem. There's Perranporth, St Agnes, Porthtowan, Portreath and Hayle to visit today. As I say, it will take all day to cover the 32 miles as I have so many stop-offs I feel like a milkman doing his round.

I have lost count as to how many pubs I have played in on this 32-mile stretch. It always was an area of tiny folk clubs in the back rooms of pubs and the feeling of DeJa'Vu today makes me nod as often as one of those stupid toy dogs people used to put on the back shelves of their cars. It's all coming back to me, the singing of traditional songs and sea shanties bellowing from tiny rooms before I went on and bored them with my own songs. The folk circuit of this part of Cornwall, just like Padstow, had its very own social scene based on homemade beer or wine and cheese at someone's house after the club closed and a willing couple to put you up for the night in their spare room. Often, you'd meet up with the entire audience for the second time that night in some kind person's house. That's exactly what it was like back in the 1960s and 1970s and nowhere more so for me than in this particular area of Cornwall. No folk singers could afford bed and breakfast, let along hotels, and we all had long journeys the following day so it just kind of went without saying that we would be offered a bed for the night. With my VW I was able to decline such offers and get my head down in privacy, at a time that suited me.

Although I don't care, I'm annoying the traffic behind as I saunter along at a snail's pace trying to not only remember the pubs I played in but also those houses where I stayed whenever the offer of a decent supper was too good to refuse.

I park up for the night, after such a busy mental day, beside Plantation Park in Hayle before the creative onslaught tomorrow of St Ives.

I reached this village by driving along Hayle River from Phillack and Copperhouse. It isn't a very big place, but it boasts an amazing history and even a by-pass, a rarity for such tiny villages. When I say river don't be misled, it's actually a large estuary that crashes into St Ives Bay further along the coast. Hayle, although going back yonks to The Iron Age and The Romans as a settlement, came of age during The Industrial Revolution in the 18th Century as a contributor to the growing tin-mining industry. The nearby furnaces were fuelled by coal from South Wales that was sailed across into Hayle port. As I said in the previous chapter, these coastal villages with their quaint harbours were far more than tourist attractions 100 or 200 years ago.

I realised today just how many memories I've stored away in the 50 years I've trod the boards around this island. Just like yourself, some I don't remember too well until a particular landmark gives me a lightbulb moment. The best way to describe it is that the fire is still there in my head, but it needs stoking from time to time.

I fully realise I'm giving more time to The West Country than other counties but it's a natural thing to do with the historic strength of the folk scene down here. This was a prominent area during my musical apprenticeship, what with its numerous clubs and festivals, so it just has to be this way. If you think this indulgent than you just wait until tomorrow when we hit St Ives. You want indulgence? You're going to get indulgence with no holds barred.

Day 46

Into St Ives we go without a man coming the other way with 7 wives. Come on now, what was all that about?

I have been here so many times I hardly know where to begin. Apparently, it's the very special light that attracts artists from afar and I get that. I park VW in the carpark behind The Sloop Inn in Wharf Road and make my way into town. I'm surprised how many other VW camper vans are gathered here. It's as though they're having a secret convention of their own, not that I'd been invited. VW looks in its element. Before heading into town proper I walk around in a giant arc to the other side of the harbour, to the lifeboat station.

I need to pay my respects because I nearly did a gig in the lifeboat station, but it was cancelled at the very last minute due to tragic circumstances. The date was 11th March 1997, and I was filming a series for WestCountry Television when news came through that the fishing boat, Gorah Lass, had gone missing and none of the crew had been accounted for. The whole town was desperate for news of the three fishermen on board. It was neither the time nor the place to making a comedy TV show so director, Gary Wicks, decided we de-rig our equipment and leave the town to mourn in private.

This 1997 disaster was the inspiration for one of my most poignant songs, The Cornish Fisherman, and I had to return today and stand quietly by the lifeboat station. It felt special, as if I knew I would return one day to do exactly this.

I spent a few days hanging out in St Ives at that time with nothing much to do but familiarise myself with this beautiful place, despite the tragedy. The Tate had just opened, and I loved spending time there, as indeed I will today, but more enchanting to me was the small, terraced cottage with the blue door where Cornish artist Alfred Wallace lived just down from The Tate. He was a Cornish Fisherman too who painted on bits of wood, cardboard boxes and anything else he could lay his hands on. He was very special, so I feel a sense of duty to visit his grave up at The Barnoon Cemetery. He's long gone now, but his colours shall never fade.

I spend the whole of day 46 in St Ives as there are so many memories to recall, not just sad and morbid memories but the many times I came here as a rookie folksinger. As I leave the town I drive around the narrow harbour road, across to the other side to The Schooner and we make our way up the hill with the harbour on our left. It's quite a climb, so much so that we look down upon the harbour and all its memories as we park up for the night at the end of the dry-stone wall that must have been a frightening job for some poor craftsman of many years ago. Once settled down for the night I sit on the wall with a can of beer and a cigarette, looking down on so much of my musical past. I knew I would return here one day and I'm so glad I finally made it.

I don't think it would be too much of an exaggeration to call St Ives the most famous fishing village or town in Britain and yet, through this 80-day journey, I now realise there are so many places just like St Ives hidden away in all the various corners of this island. It's easy to forget that, as an island, we relied heavily on a healthy fishing industry to place food on the table and harbours where ships were loaded with goods such as coal as part of our essential export trade.

As I sat here on this dry-stone wall, watching the sun sink below the horizon in romantic fashion, I can't help wondering what the hell went wrong. We're the same island we used to be and yet the fishing industry is on its knees, from here across to Lowestoft. The harbours are still here too and yet our ability to export quality goods has also diminished. Nobody expected this to happen but happen it most certainly has, so maybe nutters driving around in VW camper vans are helping the economy of the country by becoming tourists while their memories are still active enough to re-visit old haunts of their youth. Yes, I rest my case.

Day 47

Goodbye St Ives, it was great to meet up with you again but now it is time to leave with so many memories rekindled.

It seems like only the other day that I was in Cape Wrath, on the northern tip of Scotland and now I'm heading for the westernmost tip of Cornwall, Land's End. It's a total tourist trap, a location where brave people walk or cycle to from John O'Groats but I'm making the slightly shorter journey there of just a couple of miles from St Ives. The journey from John O'Groats to Land's End is 603 miles. The journey from St Ives to Land's End on the B3306 is 13 miles. So, who is the mug? I will take a look around and return back to civilisation to Penzance on the tiny road that takes in Porthcurno and Mousehole, thus avoiding the A30. However there's lots to be done before I venture back along that road, as you shall discover.

I have to be completely honest here and confess that I've never once been to Land's End before. It's never really interested me, not being the type to stand on a windswept rock to have my photograph taken beneath a signpost that points to my home far away. No, that really isn't me, but I need to visit today as part of my coastal journey or that would be cutting corners which isn't allowed.

Oh my god, this is so peculiar, the road is quiet and you see very few people for miles and then you end up at Land's End that has visitors milling around like bees around a honeypot. It makes me smile how so many of them wear yellow plastic coats and massively thick walking socks. Bright colours are the order of the day as if we are entering a Where's Wally competition. There's a gift shop where you can buy various postcards for a couple of quid that all look the same, a jagged piece of rock stretching out into the sea. Looking out in a westerly direction I'm reminded by a wooden notice that I am 3,258 miles from New York, not one of the most important noticeboards I've ever read. There aren't as many surfers here as I saw in Newquay, maybe they've all realised that America is just a little too far a voyage to attempt in a rubber suit and no engine. Many ancient mariners came a cropper here and so for them it was more than just the end of the land. Maybe they were distracted by all the tourists and lost their concentration.

I'm going to break with the tradition of our trip here by going across to The Scilly Isles and leave VW on the mainland for a well-earned rest. I'm treating it as a kind of day out, a day's holiday on our journey. No, it's not only Land's End I've never been to before, but also The Scilly Isles so it would be a nice stop off to find out more about them.

Day 48

The Scilly Isles, or The Isles of Scilly to give them their correct title, are much bigger than one would expect. They are made up of 145 islands of which 5 are inhabited and they were designated a world heritage site in 2001 so they have to be worth a visit. They are a fair distance away too, 28 miles south-west of where we were yesterday.

The island of St Agnes is the most southerly point of Britain and it's in stark contrast to Scotland's Cape Wrath with its array of colourful flowers that create an industry for the island, something that Cape Wrath is sadly not blessed with behind its MOD barbed wire.

The islands are regarded as the poorest area to live in Britain with the average annual income here of just over £15,000. My simple answer to that is who needs money when you're living in such a beautiful place far away from the rat-race. Let's be honest, what would you spend your money on anyway?

I arrive at St Mary's and there is a delightful floral scent in the air around Hugh Town. It's around 3 miles by 2 miles, maybe a fraction less. I find a stunning beach, known as Old Town Bay, and I'm quite surprised how busy the island is. It reminds me of a small version of Jersey with a fair number of restaurants and pubs. It seems like a great place to live if you're done with nightclubs and Premier League football matches. I'm equally surprised when I discover that Harold Wilson, a former Labour Prime Minister, is buried here, a far cry from Huddersfield where he was born in 1916. He was around at the same time as his Conservative counterpart, Edward Heath, who owned a yacht called Morning Cloud. Now then, of the two which would you expect to be buried here? Exactly. There's nowt so strange as folk as they say in Harold's birthplace.

From the beach, looking to the east, there are numerous offshore, uninhabited rocks. I wouldn't really call them islands myself, but I now realise why and how they can boast 145. I suppose any rock surrounded by water is an island in the true sense, but I think The Isles of Scilly push the description a little bit too far. Most of what I see are definitely rocks, no different to others dotted around our coast.

There are 9 miles of road around the edge but I'm more than happy to have given VW the day off today. He's actually resting up in Penzance, apparently where parrots come from, where I had to come to reach these islands and he'll be happy to have a snooze and cool down his oil. I take a vintage bus-ride to confirm the fact I've done the miles and I add them to my grand total. Then it's an overnight stay for me in a bed and breakfast, the owners of which have suggested I try the local fish and chips that cannot be beaten. The times we have heard that on this journey. Everywhere seems to have the best fish and chips in Britain. I'm still tossing up between Cromer, by The Pavilion, and the chippy in South Shields by The Customs House Theatre. I've eaten more fish and chips on this adventure than during my entire youth up to school-leaving age. Hey, a chip is a chip, let's face it, and most cod and haddock start out the same in the sea so it's fairly difficult to find a place, or maybe plaice, which stands out from the others. Forget that plaice gag, they're flatfish and so they can't stand out from anything at all.

It was well worth the diversion to see The Isles of Scilly in all their glory, even the little ones that didn't really have that much glory to boast about.

There's live music in a pub just down from me and I lose myself in the jovial atmosphere of island locals making their own entertainment, just as everyone used to do through the centuries. The local music is definitely tinged with the Cornish tradition and sometimes it's difficult to understand what they are singing about, but hey, my father said that whenever I played my Beatles and Rolling Stones records when I was a teenager, so perhaps nothing has changed that much after all. I shall sleep well tonight and tomorrow I will continue my journey on the mainland.

Day 49

So back to the mainland it is this morning after a hearty breakfast of grilled kippers. Why didn't I do this when I was in Arbroath? I've no idea. I should have done the same in the Northumbrian village of Seahouses too. I'm not saying for one moment I could kick myself because I tried than once and fell over, but I do regret such a remiss.

Being in the VW camper van for nearly five weeks has made my legs ache without a doubt and the break from driving did them the world of good and it did VW good too. So much so that I'm taking another coastal stroll while I'm down here on the west coast of Cornwall, to another landmark I've never visited before. This area, known as The Lizard, is south of Land's End and it's time to take a look before I finally move on and get on with the job in hand. It's a short drive of 9 miles to Helston and then it is stroll time.

Helston, a former cattle market town, is the most southerly town in Britain and it hides a musical secret. No, The Beatles never played here. We all know The Floral Dance song and this where it originated. Strangely it's not an old traditional Cornish song as one would expect as it wasn't written until 1911. Yes, it's a contemporary song from the world of traditional music.

The Lizard, our southernmost peninsula, is surrounded by The River Helford on the top and the sea on its other sides. It's designated as an area of outstanding beauty and that it certainly is, but if you're looking for sandy stretches of beach then this isn't the area for you. It's as rugged as a rugby scrum, a game they love in Cornwall by the way, so you have to be careful of your footings over the rocks. It's why crabs have shells.

The peninsula measures 14 miles by 14 miles and so is much bigger than you imagine and, basically, yes, it's a cluster of rocks that have been a danger to shipping through the years, just like Land's End. It's said there are more shipwrecks off this part of the coast than anywhere else in Britain and I can see why. They built a lighthouse here in 1752 but it obviously didn't solve the shipping problem entirely which is probably why they also have a lifeboat station too. Surely it would have all been far less trouble if the ships had sailed a little further out to sea.

All the way around Britain I have loved exploring these British outposts, places I've heard of at various times but never seen. This has been one such area, thoroughly enjoyable, far more enjoyable than it was for those unfortunate ancient mariners who must have hated the place.

I seem to have been stuck for a while in an area that offers no musical memories to me whatsoever, thus defeating the issue as to why I took this mammoth journey on in the first place. I don't even know if there are any musical venues around here. If there are they never booked me so I have no need to mention them. Without such musical references and memories I seem to be edging ever closer to the travel books of Bill Bryson and yet I mentioned at the very start of this book that this book is nothing like his. I have read all his books and worked with him with regards audio books and so I'm well aware that this nostalgic journey must not be anything like watered-down versions of works he has already written. I said at the beginning that I have far more musical and nostalgic first-hand experience of Britain that the great man and they are the very key points I seem to have neglected for the last couple of days and so it's time to get back in the VW camper van and have a drive to music venues of my past. It's what I set out do in the first place and it's time to return to my original plan or the comparisons would be well justified. To be honest, if such comparisons were ever made I know I would lose anyway. Back on the road.

Day 50

So it's no more walking for a while as I finally get a chance to drive around some old haunts in Penzance. My plan today is to say hello to some venues I have frequented in the past before heading back out on the road south and working my way along the Cornish peninsula to places more familiar to me than Land's End and The Lizard.

To the west of the harbour is the friendly Acorn Theatre where I have enjoyed a good few nights with nice audiences. I know of the folk club in The Admiral Benbow pub in Chapel Street, but it's another club I played here nearly 50 years ago at The Count House, Botallack, a little further out of town on the A30 that springs to mind and makes me smile. As is the case with most coastal towns visited on our journey the audiences through all the years have always been far more laid-back than city audiences such as Manchester or London, our Capital sprawl that is 260 miles east of where we are today. There's also an open-air theatre in Penlee Park and it was driving here that bubbled something up inside me, something I forgot all about the other day. I need to make a drastic decision.

I turn VW around and head back to the Land's End area to visit The Minack Theatre, our most famous open-air theatre and yet one that had slipped my mind. With theatrical connections all around Britain I couldn't miss out on this one and it's only a 20-mile excursion to men my error. Never having performed there it took a while to find the place.

The renowned Minack is just 4 miles from Land's End and it is listed as one of the world's most spectacular theatres. It all seems and looks very Roman as you see it rising up above the rocks with the sea all around, but it wasn't built until after the end of The First World War, it being the inspiration of a certain Rowena Cade and her gardener Billy Rawlings. The theatre actually puts on more plays than musical events such as mine, the first being The Tempest in 1929. It's quite spooky, awe inspiring, to sit here when nothing is being staged and take in the breath-taking views all around and listen to the sound of the rolling waves of the sea.

Obviously, their programme of events, around 20 per year, is seasonal and on most occasions it takes a hardy audience to sit for a few hours open to our good old British weather. The open-air theatre in Penlee Park, Penzance has a capacity of 300, but the celebrated Minack Theatre has over double that. It really is an incredible construction and I'm so pleased I turned and came back for a visit. So it's back the way I came, through Penzance and out the other side as I continue on my previously planned route.

Day 51

Good morning to you all. Another day, another dollar. I feel I have lingered long enough in this beautiful western tip of England, yet there is still much more of Cornwall to see before I head back to Devon on my journey, so it's goodbye to The Minack and The Acorn in Penzance as I finally pull myself away from this area and make my way to Falmouth.

Cornwall covers nearly 1,400 square miles and I have only driven along half of its coastline during the last few days I have been in the county. I seem to be loitering with no intent. For the next part of my journey I plan to drive around Falmouth Bay, a large watery inlet as I make my way to St Austell where I did numerous concerts at The Colosseum Theatre, situated right on the beach if I recall correctly. I take the A394 before finding the smaller coast roads instead of the more obvious A39. It really must be such a wonderful part of the country to reside, apart from the swarms of annoying tourists who jam the roads with their caravans and VW camper vans. It would drive me round the bend, watching them driving rounds these bands, narrow enough to claim a few wounded wing-mirrors.

Falmouth is situated on the mouth of The Fal Estuary, thus its name, and is not to be confused with the foul-mouthed comedians that were abundant in the 1980s and 90s.

Ah, at last another castle. I haven't seen one for a few days and was beginning to suffer withdrawal symptoms, even withdrawbridge symptoms, but this one, Pendennis Castle was part of Henry V111's defences back in the 16th Century. Beneath us now is The English Channel and being a deep-water harbour, they used to hide warships away before setting off to claim new territories within The British Empire. French ships were the easiest targets back then and the British warships used to lay in wait like freshwater pike in a lake in search of its dinner of much smaller fish.

Falmouth was also a kind of post office for The British Empire as ships would leave with mail to distant countries we had managed, somehow, to call our own. You can imagine the smuggling that went on at a time when Falmouth was allowed to be free of any customs and excise duties. Oh no, you could sail into Falmouth with far more than 200 cigarettes and a bottle of spirits hidden away in your suitcase.

My favourite theatre in Falmouth is The Princess Pavilion, a venue that was often on my tour schedule. It's only a small capacity theatre and yet I never managed to boast a sell-out concert there. Oh well, they were probably all out selling cheap fags and bottles of contraband brandy, so for that I forgive them. At least they didn't waste their money on my CDs.

From Falmouth we drive north to Penryn, a short journey of just a mile or two to the end of the estuary. Before we spin around and drive down the other side of the water it's worth taking in a little of Penryn. The one thing I've noticed on this journey is that no matter how close towns and villages are to one another, they all have their independent place in history. I suspect that some communities didn't even talk to one another too often what with transport and communication difficulties of the time. Falmouth and Penryn are no exception and although Falmouth was a vibrant harbour full of history, then Penryn had a few hidden gems of its own up its sleeve that are worth exploring whilst we are here. Cornish folk songs tell us all we need to know about what went on so, once again, there's no need to go researching.

Penryn, small as it is, was an export outlet for the vibrant tin industry of Cornwall and so it didn't really have the time to send love-letters to distant lands on mail ships, oh yes, and they sailed off to catch pilchards from here too. In terms of my own industry, I know very little about Penryn, or pilchards, and so there isn't any nostalgic waving or banter I can offer, just a pleasant drive in and out of the place, just like that freshwater pike I just mentioned.

Dropping down south on the other side of the estuary, with The English Channel firmly in our sights, we drive along The Roseland Peninsula, through the village of Portloe and on towards Charlestown, a place I have a craving to find out more about due to its classy name as Charlestown smacks, to me, of The United States of America more than Cornwall. All is about to be revealed.

Charlestown, the American version, is in Boston Massachusetts, and is also on the coast, but there the similarities end as you would suspect. Obviously, the early settlers named the place after King Charles 1 who wasn't a popular spaniel, by the way, but a prominent royal.

The Cornish Charlestown used to be called West Polmear, a tiny community in the 18th Century of just a few pilchard fishermen and their families. So, whatever happened to the good old pilchard? We rarely dine out on them these days, but this was back in the time when pilchards swam in the sea and didn't hang around in tins. But this area wasn't just pilchards, it being an important mining area for copper and tin and, later, China clay. Driving through Charlestown it isn't difficult to feel its history though. Big isn't always beautiful and it's a far more charming place than its American counterpart, I'm sure.

This excursion to the western tip of England has been a truly enjoyable time. I played so many folk clubs down here back in the day, so many I can't remember them all and I haven't finished yet. There's still more of the county to recall as we continue in a north-easterly direction up towards Devon.

Day 52

Leaving this little outpost of one kind of maritime history, I now head for another. Actually, this whole Cornish coastline is engulfed with maritime history of some form or another, associated with tin, clay, fishing and battles, to say nothing of smuggling and pasty selling.

Today I'm heading for Looe, via Fowey, it being another town very close to my heart. Other than Plymouth it has a larger population than other places I have visited over the last few days but it's still a narrow winding coastal road that will take me there.

It's good to give the camper van a run out as the journeys were short once I reached the western tip of England and I will need to put some extra miles in today to drive around The Fowey Estuary. Like other tourists I could take the famous Fowey car ferry across the water, but that would be cheating when there's a road to take.

As I get close to Fowey I spot a sign for Readymoney Cove, and any place with a name like that has to be worth a visit. There are a fair few traditional folk songs relating to Fowey but I've never heard mention of Readymoney Cove. It's a truly beautiful spot and it's brought to my notice in the local bakery that celebrated author Daphne du Maurier lived here for a while and I have to say that was a shrewd move by Daphne and hardly mysterious.

For those not too familiar with her work she is probably best known for Jamaica Inn and My Cousin Rachel. Like so many writers who find success she lived a reclusive life and she died in Fowey in 1981. The nice lady in the bakery told me not to forget to mention Rosamunde Pilcher, another local resident, and so I shall. I have heard of her but unfortunately have never read her works and know absolutely nothing about her. Anyway, Rosamunde Pilcher can now be considered mentioned. Job done. So, what about Fowey?

I'm surprised how built-up it has become over the years that have passed since I performed at the folk club here and I remember a local singer wrote a song about the connection between Fowey and the D-Day landings during World War Two. The song told of how American Marines used Fowey Harbour as an ammunition store and where it was loaded onto ships for their assault upon Omaha Beach. I kind of remember the song but I don't remember Fowey being mentioned in Saving Private Ryan.

It's 9 miles up and 9 miles back over the other side. Since waking up in Charlestown this morning I've covered 38 miles and stopped off for supplies to be taken on board and for a chinwag at Readymoney Bay. I was hoping to reach Looe today, but my grand arrival will have to wait until tomorrow as I pull over beside Whitesand Bay and get stuck into my brand-new paperback, purchased this morning, Jamaica Inn by Daphne du Maurier, whilst dining on the delightful cheese and onion pastie and custard tarts the very same lady sold me this morning. I know it sounds really odd but Cornish bakers really do know how to bake a crust. Yes, odd I know, but it's succulent and melts in your mouth.

I knew a little about Jamaica Inn through the film directed by Alfred Hitchcock. It's a murder mystery and really does take on a different feeling as I sit in the back of the camper van with my feet up on the table whilst I consume the last of my four custard tarts. There's just time to wash it all down with a can of lager before my eyes become heavy and I drop off to sleep. I feel this is the moment when I should be reaching across the bedside cabinet to turn out my bedside light before snuggling under my quilt. Unfortunately there are no such luxuries in VW so I climb into my sleeping bag and make a note to charge the batteries to my reading lamp once the engine starts running in the morning. Goodnight.

Day 53

I head for Looe a day later than expected with my head full of Hitchcock scaries. Once again, it isn't a particularly long journey, but the winding road negotiates various inlets and coves as I make my way eastward to one of my favourite Cornish locations. There are so many entertainment and musical memories to rekindle in Looe and hopefully old pals to collide with and so I shall be spending the whole day bringing it all back into my head and with luck I'll be spending a few hours of darkness in a pub I have often frequented too if I manage to meet up with a couple of old friends. Bring it on.

I've never entered Looe from the west before and so it's enjoyable to pass through the tiny hamlets and countryside that are new to me.

Through my 50 years plus on the road I have returned here many times and observed its changes. During my early visits you could drive around the town with gay abandon but this time I've had to park VW in the car park beside the bridge that joins East Looe with West Looe. It's really weird because the front bumper of the camper van is almost touching the mast of a moored-up fishing boat. Yes, both vehicles and boats park up here whilst owners go about their business and I can't think of many other carparks that can boast such a coming together of two such modes of transport.

The baby cinema, to my right as I head into town, used to be a music venue when the folk club put on special nights with the bigger names although I have to confess I wasn't one of the bigger names when I played here so long ago. I know the short cut through the weighing station where fish are stored in baskets and soon I'm walking along the sea wall watching fishermen preparing their nets for their next trip out to sea. My memories are exploding in my head as I recall a TV show I filmed here for Westcountry Television. It's not a brag, nothing like that, but it's worth mentioning because I had to do so much research to make the programme and that's how I know so much about this place. There were so many unfamiliarities to me as I drove around the top of Scotland but down here in the West Country of England it's a different ball game.

I did this very walk with TV producer Gary Wicks as we looked for interesting locations and interesting people with great stories to tell and that's how I learned of the feud between the two factions of East Looe and West Looe. Yes, Looe is a picture-postcard setting but scratching beneath the surface it's had its own history of conflict amongst its locals. You wouldn't think so but it's true.

In the 16th Century East and West Looe were twin towns joined by a bridge across the Looe River and it would seem that the two teams didn't always see eye to eye, resulting in numerous fights on the bridge. The bridge itself has an interesting history dating back to 1411 when it was first built and made of wood. The strange thing is that this first design had a small church right in the middle, surely that's a first. The bridge caught fire 25 years after it was built and the two towns were isolated from each other until they built the next one made of stone and rock. That went the way of the west too and the latest attempt to get it right was built in 1853. Whereas the earlier bridge had 15 arches to give it strength the newer version has just 7 but boasts 6 cast-iron lampposts of the same style as Waterloo Bridge in London.

I spent four days here in the 1990s making that TV show and the film crew took over an entire bed and breakfast facility in a house behind the main town close to the flat beach popular with those who indulge in water sports.

I just had to walk here and think of my time with Gary Wicks who left us a few years ago. Sadly, it has changed so much I can't locate the exact place where we stayed and so I head back into the main town, aware VW's time is up in the car park. It wouldn't have been a Welcome Break Services kind of a fine, but I have decided to stick by the rules and move along, being a good boy.

I took on supplies earlier at Sarah's Pasty Shop and am now settled down for an evening in The Fisherman's Arms, by the quay in Higher Market Street. You don't find many really good old-fashioned pubs these days but this is one such with the added bonus of some live music in the side bar. It's all well up my street, as though I hadn't ever been away. So much of our musical heritage originated with the getting together of locals in such a place, sitting around a fire in the winter months sharing a few songs and ales just as I explained before at the other end of Cornwall. There would be no folk music tradition if such places had never existed and such music is timeless and will live on forever, bucking all the various the trends of what comes and goes for the younger generations. Yes, I am in my element here. They certainly love their country music down this way with classic after Nashville classic belted out by men and women, many in lumberjack shirts. Ah forgive me, I just glanced at the poster and it advertises a night of country music. Mind you, it doesn't say which country?

Having knocked back a few during the course of the evening as I enjoyed the music I walked back to the camper van and now I can't be bothered to find a suitable place to pitch up for the night. Where it stands, right here in the road, is good enough for me. Legal or illegal, I don't really have a clue, but I will be well gone by the time the traffic-wardens come prowling the morning so it doesn't really matter.

Tomorrow promises to be an enthralling day for me as I am about to visit another old haunt and one that probably ranks as my favourite place in the whole of Britain, a place I even thought about moving to many years ago.

As a young kid raised in London I thought Cornwall was a mysterious holiday resort a million miles away from home, a land of sea and sandcastles that would never be visited again. Such a thought is understandable when you realise there were no motorways when I was a child and a trip down here would have taken 10 or 12 hours, a long way away both mentally and physically. I had no idea I would ever return to this area as an adult, but there again I never thought I would become a musician and roam the land like some wandering minstrel either. Creative bods were all raving about the delights of Cornwall in the 1960s and I became one of them myself as I grew my hair long, bought a kaftan and became a hippie. Yes, I made it halfway down here by settling in Salisbury but the temptation to go the whole hog was in my head for many years. There weren't too many folk gigs in the East End of London, especially compared to so many down here so it's hardly surprising I found Cornwall so alluring, so magnetic. I think the only thing that stopped me was my lack of funds, even in those days you couldn't just rent a place without putting down a deposit and any kind of a down-payment, whatever it was, would have been way beyond my means. That being the case I came down here as often as I could and my romance with the area grew. Tomorrow I will re-kindle that love affair and I would have driven the entire 80 days to be there.

Day 54

Bearing in mind what I said about traffic-wardens, the horrible things, I was, indeed, off bright and early and heading for Polperro. Once again, my daily mileage scheme will fall apart today as it's only 5 miles from Looe to Polperro. Well, it would have been 5 miles but it turned out to be considerably longer as I took a ridiculously narrow and winding route via Talland and Portlooe before colliding with the more obvious route into Polperro itself.

I want to make the most of my final day in Cornwall as tomorrow I will be heading back into Devon and the hustle and bustle of the big city of Plymouth. So this will be my last chance to saunter along at a sedate pace before meeting up with the short-fused commuters who will want me out of the way so they won't be late for work. My camper van will soon be in for a shock and so I treat it kindly for the last few miles of Cornish country lanes. I say I'm off to Plymouth tomorrow but it may not be the case as I have a hunch I will be hanging around here for as long as I dare.

Talland Bay, beneath Polperro, is a tiny cluster of mainly white bungalows and well worthy of a visit for those in search of some peace and quiet. The bay is small compared to others and sort of divided into two with a baby headland jutting out halfway along like a knuckle protruding from the back of a hand. As was the case in the north of Scotland I wish I had brought my paints along for the journey because this is an ideal spot to sit looking eastward across the bay and doing a quick watercolour of the water and the jagged rocks that guard the headland. It really is beautiful and worth the few extra miles involved to find it. The Talland Bay Hotel looks inviting too but I have another destination very much in my mind as I head, excitedly, into Polperro.

Not dissimilar to Looe I remember a time when it was quite acceptable to drive around Polperro but it isn't like that anymore. I park VW in the designated area and walk down into the town, I have no choice. It's all downhill with the water trickling down by the side of the road from the hills above like a small stream, but the problem with a walk downhill is that it's a walk uphill on the way back, something I man of my age doesn't really relish. Never mind, it shall be undertaken later in the day because for now there are so many re-visits on my agenda. I fell in love with Polperro half a century ago and I knew the romance wasn't over.

My eventual destination is The Blue Peter, once I get my breath back and after a few nostalgic diversions I need to make on the way. There are three pubs that bring back memories to me, The Blue Peter, The Ship and The Three Pilchards. Each will be visited during the course of this very special day.

So down the hill I stroll before I turn sharp right towards the harbour behind the row of shops. Straight ahead if I choose to not make that right turn is a hugely steep lane that leads up to an art gallery where I actually had my own exhibition 25 years ago. That's what I remember about that steep lane, the art gallery and the perfect place for a potential heart attack at most and a strained calf-muscle at least.

A tiny stone bridge takes you around the inner harbour towards The Three Pilchards, where a wonderful menu can be found. I will pop in later to say hello to old friends, but right now I'm on a mission.

The Blue Peter is stuck out, overlooking the inner-harbour to its left and the outer-harbour more or less straight ahead. Imaging walking from the pub and walking along the sea wall that separates both harbours. Now is the time for me to smile.

Getting on for 55 years ago I came here for a break with a girlfriend and I had my guitar with me, a cheap instrument that didn't object to the salt in the air. We met up with another musician and his girlfriend, whose names I can't recall, and the two of us went busking on that very sea wall. It was the only time in my life I've busked, but I loved every minute of it. We sang traditional folk songs together and we made a few quid. During lockdown of 2020 it was tempting to get out there and do it all again in Salisbury Market Square, but it's far more difficult these days. You need a licence, just like a dog.

From that musical vantage point on that sea wall, looking across the harbour to the hills above, I remembered how we wandered up that way and spent the night in a derelict shed on the edge of the cliff. Some of the shed's planks had collapsed and therefore made a perfect bed for the night. We slept soundly but when we awoke the next morning we moved the planks and discovered we'd been sleeping alongside a nest of adders. They didn't seem to mind sharing their accommodation or I probably wouldn't be here today to tell the story. Ha-ha, I wonder where Judy Silver is today.

We went busking again, having met up for breakfast with the other musician, and all was going well, so well in fact that the landlord of The Blue Peter offered us £10 each if we moved into his bar and entertained his customers. Hey, we had turned professional, getting paid for our services and we were plied with as much food as we could eat and as much drink as we could consume. Blimey, I'd even settle for a deal like that today.

As part of the same TV series for Westcountry we filmed a Cornish fishermen choir by the harbour outside The Three Pilchards. It was at night and although the floodlit setting was amazing, it was bloody freezing and so we thawed out in The Three Pilchards before more filming the next day. All these adventures were flooding back to me as I lunched in The Blue Peter before making the precarious uphill journey back up to the carpark. As I awaited my meal I noticed a poster on the wall for a live music gig the following night. Live music where I did my one and only busking session? It had to be done. None of the pub staff were old enough to remember either of my visits to their pub, hardly surprising. so I enjoyed the anonymity of someone who wanted nothing more than to sit and listen to some live music, maybe joining in a song or two.

Young people today call them open mic sessions and that's exactly what is going on tomorrow night. No paid guest, just people getting up and singing? That's no different to how the songs were handed down through the centuries. It was something I couldn't miss before leaving Cornwall.

Knowing I will be hanging around a little longer than expected I decide to dine like a lord in The Three Pilchards. It will be my first encounter with a proper China plate since way back in Essex before I set off for Suffolk, and how long ago that seems. The view from my table is glorious. As I await my steak and ale pie and fresh vegetables, a luxury on this trip, I stare out at the quaint harbour just a few yards away. I imagine that choir of fisherman just outside the pub door, floodlit as they were that night.

After my healthy meal I make my way back to VW with a heavy stomach, not a recommended condition when negotiating a stiff uphill walk. As I enter the carpark I see an adjacent Long Term Stay area. It's heaven sent as I'm exhausted, full up and lubricated with a local ale. Everything has gone so well today and it seems it's going to end in a similar way. I pull the curtains across the windscreen and I'm asleep in a few moments. I couldn't even dream of being in such a beautiful place.

Day 55

You're right, I've decided to stay an extra day in beautiful Polperro. It is hardly a chore but more a welcome, unexpected break extension. It is giving me a chance to take stock of my favourite spot and be a bit of a tourist for another day. I even thought about visiting the Polperro Model Village but I've decided against it for fear of taking on the dubious role of Gulliver treading his way in a most unwelcome manner around Lilliput. Knowing my luck I would have probably demolished a few cottages with my size 10s so I didn't want to take the risk. To be honest it isn't really my sort of thing anyway and I've always avoided it on the many previous visits and stays in Polperro. So it remained an avoidance as I chose, instead, to take a walk along the eastern cliffs and then back up the other side to see what pieces the delightful art gallery was exhibiting. Ownership had changed since my own art exhibition here and so I chose to wander round without speaking egotistical rubbish that would have meant nothing to the new owner.

I have enjoyed the evening so much. I didn't actually play as I didn't have my guitar with me, but I joined in all the chorus songs and chatted with those in the audience who recalled me filming there over 20 years ago. It brought back some great memories and it reminded me of the friendliness offered while the crew and myself stayed here for three or four days whilst we went about our annoying business.

The boats in the harbour are fewer now, much fewer, but that's the way of the world. Yes, things change as time passes but, thankfully, the heritage of our traditional folk songs doesn't and apart from my thinning hair I could have been sitting here just as I did all those years ago, singing the same songs as I did back then. Music, like art, is both ageless and timeless. It passes through the years, taking things in, until one day another traditional folk song appears and tells the story of some event or other. The 2020/2021 disaster I can guarantee, will be told through song in the future, by people who weren't even born when it came and hit us. Come to think of it they could make a movie of it too once they discover more about how the wicked enemy turned up and wrecked lives. You never know, they may make a movie about a strange man who decided to drive around the coastline of Britain whilst telling boring stories of his dubious musical past.

Day 56

Goodbye Cornwall and hello again Plymouth. It's been a while since I was last here. I thought I would be making my way by direct route to Plymouth and that was more or less the case once I had negotiated the twisty lanes out of Polperro.

It would be a short trip of 26 miles, but the pictorial changes would be extreme as we head towards the outskirts of Plymouth. When they estimate such distances they never cater for idiots in camper vans who want to take the long way round, but that's exactly what I will do.

As usual I keep tight to the coast and pass through various villages that mean I drive in a large circle before returning to a major road. The circle begins at Portwrinkle before the VW travels south-west towards Cawsand, a village twinned with Kingsand that overlooks The Tamar Estuary.

At some point we need to cross the River Tamar at Saltash on the A38 and being the history nut that I am I cannot wait to be crossing the Tamar Bridge, another testament to the amazing skills of our engineering ancestors. I love bridges as much as I love castles and other historic monuments and The Tamar Bridge is no exception. Next to this road bridge is Isambard Kingdom Brunel's sensational Royal Albert Bridge, one he built for the thriving railway industry. I must admit to it being quite an amazing distraction as I head across the border back into Devon. Work began on The Tamar Bridge in 1959 and it opened to traffic in 1961.

My musical career took me to this city many times, performing at The Theatre Royal and also presenting BBC Radio

Devon's folk programme a few years ago from their Plymouth studio.

Of course, the city is steeped in history by the shedload and it has an arty region, The Barbican, which boasts bars and restaurants in vast numbers.

Driving through Plymouth is a bit of a trial, especially when you haven't seen so many signposts and road-signs a-plenty for a week or so. Sir Francis Drake had the right idea when he came into town by ship, a smart move which gave him time to have a game of bowls while waiting for the rest of them to drive in and find somewhere to park. Apparently they even erected a huge lighthouse on The Hoe to tell his boys where they could find him.

I followed the ring road and finally found myself heading east before dropping down to the coast. To cross yet another river I stayed on the A38 for a couple of miles to Ivybridge where I stopped off at The Waterfront Theatre for a cup of coffee and a chat with the team who have both booked my performances and hosted an art exhibition of my work. It was one of the theatres I wondered if or not would survive the lockdown period but they did.

After the short break I picked up the A3121 to Modbury and then headed further south on the smaller roads towards Bigbury Bay. I drove through Kingsbridge where I'd played in their village hall before lockdown and then down to South Pool, a small hamlet where The Millbrook Inn looked tempting. I was about to head on to Dartmouth until I realised I'd accidentally by-passed Salcombe on The Kingsbridge Estuary. I apologised to the VW camper van as I turned it around and back we went. I couldn't leave it out as it gave me a memory of a trip with the

202

school. How that old coach managed to get through these narrow lanes is way beyond me, but belated congratulations to the driver. I presume he's long gone by now or he would be the oldest man who ever lived. I remember the school trip as it took a full day to reach Torquay and the last thing we wanted to do was get back in the coach again but that's exactly what we did. I have to admit as a youngster it seemed a complete waste of time as it looked the same as Torquay, the same old sand that went down to the same old sea. This time I appreciated it much more, well worth the diversion.

Day 57

It may seem strange that we've covered over three-quarters of the British coast with still another 23 days to go. Unbalanced as that may be, it's all part of the game plan. From the outset I knew the first 2 weeks would involve much longer daily drives as I ventured way up into the northern regions I didn't know too well. Equally I knew I would spend less hours behind the wheel as I visited places I knew better than others. I said at the very beginning that I didn't want to clone the Bill Bryson concept and my returning to various scenes of the crime have confirmed my desire to be completely different to the master of travel. He wasn't ignored by the Bristol folk scene like me.

I should have clocked up 4,000 miles by now and, surprisingly, I'm not too far short of that prediction, helped by the extra 17 miles I added by turning back to Salcombe to re-live that school trip. The total was obviously also assisted by having a look around some of the Scottish Isles and The Isles of Scilly. I suppose we should also include Canvey Island. I also allowed for a few days of relaxation when mileage didn't matter, as was the case as I headed from Somerset to Devon. I felt I deserved to ease off the pedal and I knew I would be feeling tired after nearly 8 weeks of driving along twisting coast-roads.

I must admit it has been quite exhausting at times and I think the contrasting days contributed to that a great deal. One day I was driving through beautiful countryside and the next I was finding my way through confusing one-way systems of towns and cities with my pedals going up down like some crazed cyclist. Then I was out the other side of those towns and cities and moving on to mysterious pastures new. What with roads I didn't know too well I needed to give full concentration, another tiredness ingredient.

So, once again, I'm taking it easy for a few days. My plan is to settle down for a good few hours in Dartmouth today. It would be a return to The Flavel Arts Centre for me plus, with a bit of luck, a ride on the steam railway on the other side of The Dart Estuary. The train journey seemed like a good idea at the time, until I realised it would take the whole day to get to Paignton and back again, a stupid, pointless idea as I would very soon be driving that way anyway in the camper van and it wouldn't be right to steal VW's thunder.

I'm not here on this trip to include train journeys anyway, no matter how relaxing and beautiful they may well be or where they may be going. For most of today I haven't been able to get mystery writer Agatha Christie out of my mind, something you will understand if you already have or are planning to take a journey on The Dartford Steam Railway in the future. This is that lady's patch and her books come to life here. Just think, had this lady not been born just up the road in Torquay then there would have been no Hercule Poirot and nobody would ever have gone to watch The Mousetrap.

It's often stated that Agatha Christie lived at Greenway House on the banks of The River Dart, a stunning estate now looked after by The National Trust, very close to where I am right now, but that isn't quite true. It was actually her holiday home. Despite all that I think it's worth noting for both you and I, mainly myself I feel, that Agatha Christie had had first six books rejected by publishers as not good enough. Didn't the same thing happen to JK Rowling up in Edinburgh? Suddenly I feel in good company and if you ever fancy trying to write a book yourself there's every chance you'll be in similar company. Hey, they both got there in the end so I reckon we stand an outside chance too. Just don't put all your eggs in one basket, especially if you've given up writing and taken up chicken farming.

Day 58

Back in the camper van and north I go towards my final destination of the day, Torquay. I enjoyed two summer seasons in Torquay of 9 weeks each in the 1980s so I would have played The Princess Theatre over 100 times, no less. For a while it was a second home to me, staying at The Warren Park Hotel with its stunning views across the sea.

I take the A3122 from Dartmouth and join the A381 for my 24-mile drive to Brixham, Torquay's next-door neighbour. Taking the B3205 and boarding the ferry would have reduced travelling time by 17 miles but there was a coast road that avoided the ferry and so it had to be done to keep to my usual rules.

Brixham, halfway to Torquay along what they call The English Riviera, has grown beyond all recognition since I first came here. It used to be a simple drive down to the fish market area but now it's too complicated to even try and so I park in the municipal carpark and continue my journey on foot. It has always been a haven for the bigger, deep-sea trawlers and despite the decline in the fishing industry it remains that way. It may be noisy and busy but Brixham is a genuine fishing town, but yes, it still operates as such. It also has annual music festival that I've never played at and therefore know very little about, but maybe more interesting it has a pirate festival too when many of its residents dress up as pirates and walk around the town with a patch over one eye and a toy parrot on their shoulder. Why? I have no answer but I bet it's fun It could only happen in Britain couldn't it?

My additional connection with Brixham, irrelevant to the trip but I fee worthy of note, is that once did a gig on a T Class Royal Navy submarine, HMS Torbay. It was the longest, thinnest audience I've ever worked to and I banged my head half a dozen times during each song. As I say, it has little to do with this expedition but I'm sure you'd mention it too had you performed underwater to a bunch of submariners.

This part of the West Country, the same as Cornwall, thrives on tourism and it had a bumper time when all flights to holiday destinations abroad were cancelled in 2021. The M5 was gridlocked for weeks and the smaller roads impassable due to the weight of traffic. Brixham was no exception as people flocked to the area from all corners of a handcuffed Britain. I must stress here before I mention it as it isn't my kind of thing, but there's a replica of Drake's Golden Hind sailing ship moored here and is apparently popular with marauding tourists who climb on board for a few quid. I don't really get it but if it brings much-needed cash to the area then who am I to comment? At least The Victory at Portsmouth is the real thing.

I thought about spending more time looking around the place, as I did with my parents so long ago, but I decided to be on my way, earlier than expected, but not to my final destination because next to Torquay is the town of Paignton where I truly performed at its zoo to help raise funds for a new elephant enclosure. It just has to be on my agenda to pop in and see how it's all going. Looking after all the animals with no income in recent times, I mean the zoo having no income and not the animals, must have been a scary time but somehow they managed it. Of course they did, the British are the greatest animal lovers in the world so no harm could come to our four-legged friends.

When not in summer season down the road I occasionally performed at The Palace Theatre in Paignton, built in 1890 and resembling The Shepherds Bush Empire in London. It's much smaller than its Torquay counterpart, around 400 seats I would guess, and it makes for a nice intimate evening of music and fun. I may be wrong but how I saw it at the time was that The Princess in Torquay relied on tourists and holidaymakers whereas The Palace catered very much for the locals when the season calmed down. Come to think of it I'm sure I'm wrong as holidaymakers went to Paignton too.

My respects paid to the zoo and the theatre it was time to complete my journey with a 4-mile drive along the B3201 and the A3022 into Torquay. At this point Torbay swings away to the right and the lights of the town and its promenade can be seen way in the distance.

It's a nice drive along the promenade, with the new Conference Centre on the left and The Princess Theatre on the right, but I carry on past both to reach the marina and sweep around towards The Imperial Hotel, a route I took when I performed each year at The Babbacombe Theatre, further along the coast. Unlike the other theatres here The Babbacombe nestles amongst private houses, not suitable for an overnight in the camper van so I drive through Babbacombe itself and make my way along the cliffs to Maidencombe, a perfect place to rest.

My times in Torquay, during summer seasons, were always hectic, far more so than most coastal towns, mainly because I drove around the town during the 9 weeks doing interviews, visiting hospitals, appearing on the local radio station and the local newspaper offices, plugging the shows with great regularity. Just the once was never enough as new tourists arrived each week or fortnight whilst others left. It was a rotational thing. That said, Torquay is now behind me as I settle down in Maidencombe. Goodnight.

Day 59

I woke this morning with the desire to visit Totnes, a town well known for its alternative this and alternative that. And so it is that I have made a daytrip, you could even call it a pilgrimage, to this quirky Devon town where my VW camper van will not look at all out of place.

The A385 is a straight drive west of just 9 miles but I'm doing the lanes as usual, through Cockington and dropping down on the A380.

Many years ago on TV I described Totnes as the place, the hub if you like, where people who wanted to be different found peace and solitude. The big problem was that everyone who wanted to be different all looked the same with their kaftans and sandals so none of them were any different at all. Their local paper gave me a right mauling when I said on my TV show that Totnes is the only place in Britain where, if there is a bad road accident, someone will fight through the crowd shouting 'make way, I'm an aromatherapist.' They hated me for that, so much so that I was banned from ever performing in the town again. Because of that harsh sentence this is the first time I've been back here for years.

The truth is I loved the place, so much history lurking behind its smell of petunia oil and incense. Yes, I just had to come back, but with my baseball cap pulled down to my eyes and sunglasses hopefully hiding my criminal identity.

They built a castle way back in the year of 907 and you can bet your life it had a natural health shop and another that sold scented candles. If it had still been operative when my TV show was filmed at The Royal Seven Stars Hotel they would have locked me up in that castle and thrown the key into The River Dart.

They say that the police in Totnes are not taught to fight crime as there isn't any. Instead they are taught the art of full body massage. To be honest I can't see the pleasure in being stretched out naked on a couch while a woman in a policewoman massages my back. Can you????

Members of the New Age community muster here during the colder months when there are no festivals to attend elsewhere. That very fact gives rise to another of my rather strange thoughts, why do old age travellers have new caravans and new age travellers have old caravans?

Anyway, if you want to witness the alternative life of everyone who's the same as everyone else then this visit is a must. Just don't attend the mindfulness bongo drum sessions if you had a few too many the night before.

In 1646, Oliver Cromwell met with his foe here at The Guildhall to discuss some kind of settlement and the table he sat around with Thomas Fairfax is still there to this day. I sat at that very table and it sent shivers down my spine. The Guildhall and all its history alone is well worth a visit to the town. Once a prison and then a magistrate's court, it has remarkable stories of its own.

So how alternative is Totnes? Well, in 2007 it became the first place in Britain to create its own currency, The Totnes Pound. I would consider that to be fairly alternative. The amazing thing is it worked, which makes me wonder if the rest of Britain missed a trick when considering the modern-day political policy of robbing from the poor to give to the rich.

Westminster should be moved to Totnes and Robin Hood should become Prime Minister, which should sort it out.

I have another thought that may make you ponder. Totnes, a place that doesn't court hi-tech progress and development is where hi-tech whizz-kid Charles Babbage went to school before he went off to Cambridge. Yes, Charles Babbage, he who invented the computer. It really is strange how the modern and the traditional collide so many times on our island.

It's time to leave Totnes as I head back on the A381 towards the Torbay coast, but it was a great memory for me to return to a place where I would have been hung, drawn and quartered a few centuries ago. In this crazy modern world that we all think at times seems to be heading in the wrong direction it's quite reassuring to confess a saw a man sitting cross-legged on a traffic island bashing away on an old acoustic guitar causing no harm to anyone. I have to admit to totally admiring him. He probably doesn't know too much about Brexit, just like our politicians who don't know too much about it either. It kind of makes you think doesn't it? It was well worth the 18-mile round trip this morning.

VW was admired and I was ignored, just how I wanted it to be. When I filmed here 25 years ago I found the whole town somewhat amusing, but I'm now well and truly converted, almost jealous of the way they live here, confirmation that old age does indeed calm you down and think differently. I mean to say, where else would a post office sell massage oil? They now have my total respect. Blimey, next I reckon I'll be getting a plane over to Woodstock.

I think I'll have another sleep-over in the Torquay area tonight before heading upstream to Exeter. It may just be a coincidence but I feel very relaxed and chilled-out right now so perhaps the population of Totnes do have it right. I really enjoyed the trespass and I wish them all well. I'd rather not toast them with a glass of elderberry wine but, yes, I wish them well just the same.

Day 60

Back to normality today, whatever that is. My ancient VW camper van was sorry to leave Totnes, having mingled with so many of its brothers, sisters and distant relatives.

The direct route mileage from Torquay to Exeter is 23 miles but we are taking a far more picturesque route to the right of the main road. It's yet another area that attracts holidaymakers in their multitudes and so the volume of traffic is always highly unpredictable, although hopefully most stick to the main road and get to their destinations as quickly as possible thus leaving the lanes fairly empty for people like me.

Teignmouth and Dawlish are too beautiful places worth a visit along the coast and the A379 takes us there.

Teignmouth is, not surprisingly, situated on the mouth of The River Teign. It's a pretty place but it also has a historic structure of great interest, Shaldon Bridge. It was built in 1827 and at the time became the longest wooden bridge in England with its 34 arches. It was over 1,500 feet long but it needed some design ingenuity as it needed to be a swing-bridge kind of construction so that ships could pass through. That was quite something to build in the early 19th Century and it proved to be an astonishing success, but only for a short time because it collapsed 11 years later.

20 years on from there and we turn to our old friend Isambard Kingdom Brunel who, in 1846, built a railway line that literally ran a fair few miles beside the sea wall, opening up trade by making the small coastal villages more accessible. It's incredible to think that so many of Brunel's great engineering works still stand to this day. If he could come back today he

would be a proud man for sure. Oh yes, he'd love to catch a train down to here to see again his incredible feats of engineering still in operation, train cancellations permitting of course. It's a shame he didn't invent something that cleared fallen leaves off tracks too.

My journey to Dawlish and Dawlish Warren means a small circular trip before taking the B3182 to Exeter. Although we do not need to go quite that far to negotiate the River Exe Estuary we will still need to drive halfway there if we are to avoid the M5 and its eternal queues of traffic. There's good reason why I'll add the few miles to the day's journey, in fact there's a few good reasons. Firstly, my daughter Rosie was born in Exeter and, secondly, I spent numerous days, weeks and months in The BBC's Exeter studios making radio shows. So, being in the area, it seems right to pop in and say hello to the staff who helped me make those programmes.

I always preferred recording in Exeter more than Plymouth as the studios were much smaller and friendlier than its Plymouth counterpart, plus the fact Exeter is a darn sight closer to my home in Salisbury.

I've never approached Exeter from this direction before, via Exminster and Shillingford Abbot on my way to Topsham, so it's hardly surprising I've managed to lose my way a good half a dozen times as I honour my pledge to not use a Satnav. Arrogantly, I thought I knew this area well enough to not even bother opening my road atlas but oh how wrong was I. I have cursed that decision a few times this morning before it all made sense by discovering the radio studios had moved to Exeter College. No wonder I couldn't find them.

Next to where the studios used to be is a bed and breakfast that became a regular haunt of mine and it was nice to see the proprietors once again, made all the more enticing by the fact I knew I'll have fresh kippers and a poached egg in the morning.

There's much to know about Exeter and tonight I'm reading all the leaflets that have been left by the front door of this bed and breakfast establishment to discover as much as I can. For starters, Exeter Guildhall is the oldest civic building in Britain. They tried putting gigs on there a few years ago and I remember my performance there well as The Romans made no allowances for getting pa systems through narrow doors. Ha, so they didn't know everything after all.

The Royal Clarence is the oldest hotel in Britain, built in the 15th Century way before hotel reception staff refused to talk to you until they swiped your credit card and down the road is where the last woman in Britain was tried for practicing witchcraft. I think I went there once for a driving offence, but not from driving the plodding camper van I'm using on this adventure.

I have no idea the miles my VW has clocked up in its long lifetime but id doesn't really matter because VW camper vans never die, they just slow down like the rest of us.

JK Rowling studied here at Exeter University and I'm hoping, by coming here, that some of her incredible publishing success will rub off on me with regards this attempt. The fine lady has been mentioned many times during this trip so it seems only right that she is given yet another mention at the place where she leant to become such a literary genius. In terms of music they can also boast Coldplay's Chris Martin and

217

show business can do the same regarding the one and only Tommy Cooper, Britain's greatest-ever entertainer, who moved here at the age of 3, presumably with his parents. There used to be an art mural dedicated to him on the side of a bridge near to his family home in Fords Road. It would have made for a 'must do' drive today, but it was vandalised and painted over. So sad, so very sad.

Day 61

Today, kippers and poached eggs consumed and digested, I head east as the Devon coast stretches way off to the right. To head that way I take the A376 back to Topsham on the northern side of the Exe Estuary. The roads then soon narrow greatly, swerving around various watery inlets as the county heads further east. To take in all aspects of this particularly tranquil part of the coast I need to head for and reach Exmouth as my mission today.

It's only a 13-mile journey from the hustle and bustle of Exeter, but I'm making a day of it to allow lunch at The Exmouth Pavilion, a venue I played so many times during my TV career. The tiny cafeteria to the right-hand side of the theatre is cosy and friendly and there's no better view as I choose to sit on the patio outside with home-made lasagne and a pot of tea, a proper pot of tea. Don't you hate a cup of hot water with a tea bag in the saucer next to a tasteless biscuit you didn't want in the first place? Exactly, this is a proper teapot with proper tea inside, such a delightful change. It's a classic idea of a modern idea not working, a bit like the nouveau cuisine era when you paid a small fortune for a pea, a mushroom and half a sardine on a plate the size of the Wimbledon shield.

I often sit and wonder, as I sit and relax like this, what this area was like before it became a popular retirement area for the elderly. It's all very peaceful nowadays but it never used to be like that. Because of its wet and windy location, along with its shallow waters, it took a while for Exmouth to develop as a port but it still has a place in history once it all got under way as Sir Walter Raleigh often sailed from here in the 16th

Century. Things picked up even more in the 18th Century when a craze developed regarding the healing qualities of its salt water and visitors suffering from all sorts of ailments flocked here rather than over to volatile France, a country that still had regular skirmishes at sea with Britain. All I can say is the belief in the healing qualities of salt worked for The Romans so why blame them for giving it a go in Exmouth?

I had originally planned to spend tonight here, in the car park across the road from The Pavilion Theatre, close to the water's edge, but I've changed my mind. Being so flat, there isn't really that much to see or do in Exmouth, yes it's a beautiful spot but it isn't really feeding my imagination. The theatre doesn't look any different to when I performed here 10 years ago and there isn't much else here to hold my attention and so I decide to move on.

It's time to move along the coast a few miles to Budleigh Salterton where I shall drop anchor and bed down for the night.

Day 62

Good morning Budleigh Salterton, East Devon, on the B3178. Let's begin by trying to find out from a local how on earth they came with such a swanky name for such a small village. Situated on the River Otter the derivation of its name is quite simple because years ago, just like in Exmouth, they gathered sea salt in pans before the tidal river spilled into the sea. Strangely, it was a similar method that caught eels in traps as they migrated and locals think that's how their ancestors came up with the idea. I thought it would be far more sophisticated than that, but not so. It was a salt town which explains the second part of its name.

As for Budleigh there isn't anything mysterious about that either. Many villages and hamlets of Britain were named after the families that first lived there and this name came from a family living in Bodley, which in turn is a derivation of the word leigh which means clearing.

So there you have it, a simple explanation of a name that, historically, isn't anywhere near as exciting as it sounds. Time to move on along this flat coastline towards the sleepy town of Sidmouth, home of Britain's most prestigious traditional folk music folk festival.

It's a shame it's against the rules to venture inland because Ottery St Mary hosts a remarkable annual event that just cannot be matched. Every year on November 5th barrels of burning tar are carried through the town on participant's shoulders. It's some kind of fertility tradition I would imagine and a few years ago I presented a TV show from there as the runners raced through the market square, scattering the terrified spectators as they sped through. We set up a studio in a room above the butcher's shop in the square and it proved to be a perfect vantage point to witness one of the most dangerous things I've ever seen. Sparks fly everywhere and burning tar trickles down necks and shoulders of the crazy runners. The most amazing thing is that they are always over-subscribed for willing volunteers. I reckon it ranks alongside the Pamploma bull chase through the streets, a far cry from East Devon. And it isn't just adults that take part, with young children belting through with smaller barrels on fire above their young heads. It's total madness, a spectacle indeed, but something that I wouldn't dream of doing myself. As for letting my children take part, no chance.

Meanwhile, back in Sidmouth, some would say the very home of traditional folk music, I visit the Dairy Shop in Church Street where they make their own gin from local ingredients such as seaweed. I came to the folk festival here a few times and performed even more times at the Seaton Holiday Village just down the road and all I can say is thank heavens there wasn't a gin shop here back then because I don't think I would have found the stage.

Sidmouth Folk Festival rarely book singer/songwriters such as me because it's a far more traditional event of both song and dance with performers from all around the world taking part. It was the brainchild of The English Folk Dance and Song Society in 1955 and it's gone from strength to strength. Even in these nervous, troubled times, Sidmouth can boast so many of its attractions being outdoors in the fresh air. Every year, during the first week of August, over 700 events take place and much local beer is consumed. It's had its tough times but it lives on.

The onward journey from Sidmouth has brought me just a little way along the coast to Beer.

Anyone interested in model railways will know Beer is the home of Pecorama, makers of model railway bits and pieces, from track, to buildings, to coaches and engines. As we drive into the village the Pecorama factory is to the right, down Mare Lane, but a left turn takes us down the hill into the village itself.

The tiny bay is straight ahead and when I say tiny I mean really tiny. Instead of driving straight into the sea I've taken the right fork up the steep hill to a pub that I have frequented many times, one I rate as one of the best servers of pub food anywhere in the country. Welcome to The Anchor Inn. The camper van struggled to get up the hill as I found myself running out of gears but we got here in the end and the pub landlord has given me permission to sleep in the van overnight, just by the side of the pub. thus giving me one of the most beautiful early morning views I could ever wish to see tomorrow. A perfect location in more ways than one I would suggest.

While they prepare my meal, I sit on the stone wall outside and look down on the harbour, just like I did in St Ives, but this is oh so different. I'm so high up and the bay is so small it really does look like one of Pecorama's models from way up here.

Although I will spend the night here in perfect splendour I won't be hanging around too long in the morning as I need to visit The Donkey Sanctuary at Slade House Farm, a place that has improved the lives of literally thousands of relieved animals by rescuing them from awful and cruel situations in many cases. We are a nation of animal lovers and The Donkey Sanctuary here is the proof as animals arrive here from all over Europe. Once I've paid my respect to the Sanctuary I will drive along the Jurassic Coast to Lyme Regis.

Day 63

It's a bit up hill and down dale this morning and I don't think VW is enjoying it too much. Branscombe is more or less the start of the Jurassic Coast and it's more popular with the locals than with tourists as it's hidden away and reached by a steep road that I'm sure rivals Everest in terms of gradient and danger. Tourists wouldn't even know it's here. In truth there isn't too much here anyway, other than some peace and quiet, but it's a great way of checking the brake pads on your car, although be it at your peril. Should it all go well, and I survive, I will soon be in Lyme Regis.

We drive into Lyme via Sidmouth Road, sweeping right as we make our way downhill into the town. Before reaching the town centre we turn right and head down to The Cobb, the town's harbour wall made famous in the movie The French Lieutenant's Woman. Coincidentally, the author of the film, John Fowles, who wrote the book in 1969, lived on the corner by the carpark.

In more recent times Kate Winslett starred in the movie, Ammonite, the story of Mary Anning, the woman who locals claim began the famed fossil hunting here. Mary lived in the town and to our left as we leave the bottom of the town is Anning Road, such is the connection.

I lived in Lyme Regis for nearly 9 years and only moved because it was too far away from London where I was working most of the time. The making of the film was an amazing experience and many of my friends had paid extras work. We seldom saw Jeremy Irons during filming but Meryl Streep mixed with the locals and drank in The Standard, a delightful and approachable woman.

Living in Lyme I was always intrigued as to why they never made more of their history additional to the fossils found on Charmouth beach. Jane Austen stayed here and wrote of the town in Pride and Prejudice, Joseph Lister practiced medicine in a small surgery known as The Gables and comedian Peter Cook was brought up just up the road in Uplyme. All that amazing stuff and yet the town seems to choose to keep it all a secret.

Down into the town centre and out the other side on the A3052, past the famous fossil shop to my left and The Marine Theatre hanging off a cliff to my right I sweep left at The London Tavern, we are so close to the sea that we need a windscreen wiper to remove the spray. Then it's up past the football field and golf club and on to The Hunters Lodge where I will stay overnight, allowing me to look up my many friends in the town and share a few beers. This is a nostalgic moment that I've wanted to do for many years.

The Hunters Lodge is on the A35 which I have managed to stay away from as I hugged the coast. Sitting here I see how much the place has changed. The road leads to Axminster to the west but we will be heading east towards Charmouth when we get back on the road. The A35 is now busier and much wider than it used to be, now a main arterial road that carries piles of traffic to the West Country. No sooner would I have I joined it tomorrow but I'll be leaving the A35 to wriggle my way along by the sea as I travel further east from East Devon into Dorset, Thomas Hardy country.

I feel this part of the southern coastline is the beginning of my homeward journey, my last lap, back to Southampton where it all began. There's still a fair way to go and lot more theatres to pay my respects to before journey's end, but it's a relatively straight run not unlike the straight road along the beach of South Shields that led me to the end of my Great North Run. Yes, I sense I'm on the home straight now and that may be a strange thing to say as I still have over 2 weeks to go of my 80 days on the road. Fear not, there are plans afoot that will make me aware I will need to finish on time.

Day 64

It was great to re-visit Lyme Regis after so many years, but I need to continue my journey if, despite what I just said, I'm going to complete my plan in 80 days. Turning off the A35 I drive into Charmouth where my daughter Polly went to school.

Driving into the small village leads to a dead end and a carpark by the sea where the country's most incredible fossil shop is situated, although there's very little else. We're not talking Blackpool here. In actual fact it isn't really a shop as you imagine it to be, but more a giant shed full of little things that are millions of years old. I can't begin to tell you what a total joy it is to be around objects that are slightly older than me for a change, although I must admit I often feel washed up myself at times, just like them.

VW rests up in the carpark as I get a coffee in the small refreshments shop next to the fossil shed. I open the sliding door on the side of the van and drink my coffee as I watch the multitudes of fossil hunters dotted along the beach, ignoring the rain, from Charmouth to The Golden Cap, all hoping they find something that's been hiding away for millions of years. It's a dangerous area due to serious and regular cliff erosion but that doesn't seem to deter them from tapping away with their tiny hammers, the kind that my dad used to break Brazil nut toffee when I was a kid.

And so my nostalgic excursion to good old Charmouth has now come to an end as I pull out of the carpark, passing The Memorial Hall on my left where I performed at The Charmouth Folk Festival a couple of years ago and my daughter Polly's old school building on my right, before returning to the

A35 and turning right to drive further into Dorset on my way back to Southampton. From a selfish, personal point of view, this has been one of the most enjoyable days of the tour for obvious reasons. The times I've sat in my car in this tiny road, picking Polly up from school, although I should add the school she went to isn't there anymore, irrelevant but true.

The traffic on the A35 reminds me we're well and truly back in the modern world. It's a straight section of road and cars are driving faster than they should be, something I haven't managed in the VW camper van, but I'm on the move. There is no coastal road as such and so I have to put up with the noise and antics of modern drivers for a few miles before I veer off to coastal backwaters further down the road.

Day 65

Today we're off to Bridport, a town situated where The River Brit empties out into Lyme Bay. Like Lyme Regis back along the coast it has a pretty, working harbour known as West Bay. The town is known for its rope-making industry dating back to 1211 when King John ordered them to make as much rope as they could for the warships.

When driving through Bridport I'm amazed by the width of the road and I've discovered the reason. The street was used to dry the ropes that had been made in local gardens and that process often took a few weeks, dependent upon the weather. When ships returned from war the damaged ropes were replaced and the old ones were sold off, thus the term money for old rope.

Away from war connections Bridport also became a net-making centre, an art-form for by all accounts, creating a service for the local fishing boats and quite possibly old grannies that wanted to put their hair up in a bun.

By the town hall I turn right into South Street. To my left is The Arts Centre, the venue for The Bridport Folk Festival where I performed before lockdown. Bridport embraces its local folk music and during the weekend of the festival there are additional musical events in the streets, just like a small version of Sidmouth. We head for the sea by driving to the end of South Street, but I switch my attentions back to West Bay.

The interesting thing about West Bay, just over a mile from Bridport, is that it has been moved twice due to weather damage and the harbour silting up too much to house marine traffic, thus re-building it by the shelter of East Cliff. I may be wrong but surely this can be the only fishing harbour that has been moved twice. And if that isn't unique enough, surely it's a one-off situation that it has two piers too when much bigger sea towns are content with just one. Yes, there's certainly uniqueness surrounding this area.

It's also a good place to take in supplies for the rest of journey, particularly Moores Biscuits who have been baking since 1880 and have the exclusive recipe of the famous Dorset Knob biscuit, a favourite of Thomas Hardy. Even if you don't like the biscuits they're worth buying for the arty tins they come in, perfect for pencils and paintbrushes. In the days I lived in the area they were based on the A35 itself, a few miles to the west of Bridport in Morecombelake, but now they are bedded down in St Andrews Road. Easy to park and easy to spend money sums up their new premises.

Rather than take the obvious route out of Bridport I drop down south, close to the sea, towards Abbotsbury and then hopefully on to Weymouth by the end of the day.

Before heading off east on the B3157 I drop down to the Abbotsbury Swannery, the only place in the whole world where the public are invited to walk through a colony of nesting mute swans. It's a beautiful experience but that wasn't the case when the monks built their monastery here in 1040 and kept swans as tasty dishes. For 500 years those things lived in fear of being eaten, and we wonder why swans don't like us?

Although Weymouth is in our sights we linger beside this part of The English Channel a little longer to visit Chesil Beach, made famous by the Barnes Wallis bouncing bomb rehearsals in preparation for The Dam Busters attack on Germany. I'm hoping, just like me, you've heard of Chesil Beach but don't know too much about it. Ok, if you've ever seen a bag of shingle for sale in a garden centre, then Chesil Beach is a great big version of that, 18 miles long and 660 feet wide. The sea has piled it up high too and it's a sight to behold as it looks man-made. At the southern end of the beach, at the Victoria Square Roundabout on the A354, I drive to the Isle of Portland. It's amazing how much history is attached to this tiny speck of land that sticks out precariously into The Channel and I intend to find out more in the morning.

Day 66

It's Chesil Beach that links The Isle of Portland to the mainland. The island is 4 miles long and 1.7 miles wide. Yes, it's tiny but it has to be included on our coastal journey. It's history? Well, they used Portland stone to build St Paul's Cathedral and The Cenotaph Memorial in Whitehall in London. That's a fairly impressive start. Portland Harbour is one of the biggest man-made harbours in the world. It has Portland Castle that Henry V111 demanded to be built in 1539 to defend the Isle from the French and there's a town in Oregon, The United States of America that bears its name. Oh and Portland sand is the most suitable for golf course bunkers and is therefore much in demand. That's not a bad boast for 4 miles by 1.7 miles of land is it? Oh yes, and there's an HM Prison in Grove, one of Portland's few villages, plus the renowned Portland Bill headland at the southern tip of the Isle. Let's add the fact that The Romans also lived here for a while. Well of course they did. I've learnt in the last couple of months that The Romans lived more or less everywhere.

There's far more to see and hear about then I had ever expected as I drive around this short distance and the 4 island villages of Castletown, Grove, Easton and Weston.

As I prepare to leave over Fleet Lagoon I'm warned by a local that, by the way, Portland cement has nothing to do with Portland, other than the fact the name was nicked because it's the same colour as Portland stone when it sets. Phew, thank God I didn't get that wrong. I just wouldn't have slept soundly tonight had he not told me.

I look across to Chesil Beach and I can't help thinking once more about those bombers practicing for a mission which turned fortunes during The Second World War. I sit and ponder until I fall sound asleep, overcome with the tiny place's vast history. You could write a book about this place, but hang on a moment, I think that's what I seem to be doing.

Day 67

It's cold and damp in VW this morning so it's time to start the engine, get the heater on and finally make my way to Weymouth on the mainland. Weymouth is one of those places where you think you've arrived and then there's a second part to it.

As I leave the A354 behind to take to the smaller roads the B3156 becomes the B3155 and Portland Bay to my right suddenly becomes Weymouth Bay although it's the same section of water. Compared to where we've been over the last couple of days, Weymouth is a big place and it was the pride of Victorian England.

I've performed at Weymouth Pavilion a good few times, probably a dozen, and you find it by driving to the promenade and turning right at the clocktower before you end up in The English Channel, but over 300 years ago there was an alternative theatre, known as the Theatre Royal and it was the first purpose-built theatre outside of London. Before you dare to suggest, no I didn't open it. So yes, there's a history of the arts here and one of our greatest authors, Thomas Hardy, lived here in Wooperton Street, quite possibly far from the madding crowd.

The 2012 Olympic Games brought many changes to Weymouth when it became its sailing venue, including the new road that has brought me down to the south side of The River Wey before entering Weymouth proper. That was a hell of a hair-pin bend as I came down the hill. Luckily I had the brakes checked before this journey began. Then it was over Swannery

Bridge, right at the roundabout to King Street and bingo, I am finally in business.

There are numerous signs for ferries, a reminder that Weymouth has always been a vibrant port. Exports leave and imports arrive, the biggest uninvited import being The Black Death that arrived in Weymouth from France in 1348. Apparently, it killed half of Britain's population and there's even a plaque here confirming this is where it arrived on a merchant ship from Calais. I think I prefer to see the plaque depicting the home of Thomas Hardy.

Although the ferry signs are still here it would appear that the cross-channel services hit the buffers a few years ago. However, it gave me an idea this morning. I'll tell you all about my lightbulb moment when we reach Poole as it all depends on how we are doing for time.

Weymouth has an amazing music scene, a truly amazing music scene, and it's difficult to find a pub that doesn't have live music in some form or other. It makes me wonder why, over 50 years, I never got to play a folk music venue here, never performing in the town until I played The Pavilion. Oh well, best I think about moving on to pastures new, but not right now. I'm spending the night in the carpark beside the old railway terminal, adjacent to the theatre, and then I'll be saying goodbye to Weymouth in the morning. 144,000 British and American troops sailed from here to take part in the D-Day Landings and sadly, many of them never returned. My journey tomorrow isn't fraught with such dangers. I'm heading to Lulworth Cove, not France.

With what happened recently regarding lockdown, I should point out that cars and camper vans weren't the only means of transport parked up here in Weymouth. Cruise ships were frustratingly moored up here waiting to get back to sea once things improved. They were anchored offshore in lines, like skittles in a bowling alley, for well over a year and, being a hardened cruise entertainer with 30 or 40 such voyages under my belt I thought, tomorrow it would be fun to jump on board one of the very few that still remain, to give you an insight into completely different world of entertainment. Yes, let's take a day out to board a cruise ship and have a look around behind the scenes.

Cruising is one of the most popular holiday ideas for The British so I'll tell you more about the floating holiday camps that were sitting here in Weymouth, waiting for action stations.

Day 68

All aboard my hearties for something different.

A world cruise can last up to 90 days, 10 days longer than my own trip around Britain, but I have just one day to re-taste the splendour of a cruise ship after being away from them for so long, not as a passenger but as an entertainer. A cruise suits both those who wish to socialise and make new friends on the salty brine along with those who choose to be more reclusive and hang around in their cabins. I have to admit to being the latter. Sitting on a balcony and watching the world go by suits me just fine.

During the recent lockdowns some cruise ships went around Britain's coast, just like we are in the camper van, not being allowed to enter international waters until the globe's health improved. I shudder to think how much they must have spent on fuel going around our island, much more than the camper van, assuming of course they could get hold of any in this new precarious climate we seem to be living in now.

Today, the ship I'm boarding is going nowhere as, just like me, they're having a day off. It's nothing more than a guided tour by one of the ship's crew but I thought it would make a change. The reception and it's sweeping staircase, waterfall and chandeliers smack of decadence the minute I come on board. The shops sell top of the range goods including original paintings, designer clothes and jewellery that isn't reproduction. It's all very well but I'm already missing my mate VW like mad in this bizarre maritime world.

I'm taken to the ship's bridge and I see nothing other than long banks of computers and flashing lights. There's no rear-view mirror, no polo mints, no ashtray or glove compartment and no air-freshener dangling from the windscreen. There's not even a great big wheel for the captain to spin in the hope of avoiding rocks.

It's all so alien to me now and I'm even more homesick now for my camper van as I'm slowly losing interest in my hi-tech surroundings and the crew member's running commentary, kind as he is to have invited me. You know those moments when you think you've made a bit of a mistake and you wish you were somewhere else? That's where I am right now and I want to get back onto dry land as soon as possible. I can see the carpark in the distance, where I left VW, and I almost hear it calling out to me. Yes, I thought it was a good idea at the time but I admit I was wrong.

Having said all of that the first-class lunch is most welcome to someone who has been in and out of baker's and fish and chip shops for a few weeks. Food on cruise ships is second to none and I tuck into my served cuisine like someone in the Oliver musical, but I feel guilty, so much so I almost feel like sorting out a doggy bag for the camper van.

It was nice to be given a little VIP treatment as one of their entertainers and I thought it would be a welcome diversion to what I've been up to but all I can think of right now is getting back on the road and continuing my dream trip, just like the ship's crew were until just a short time ago.

The newspapers kept saying it wouldn't be too long before the big, paralysed hotels of the seas would be back in regular service around the world, no longer feeling like casualties lined up in a hospital ward, looking and feeling really sorry for themselves but their wait was far longer than they expected. They longed to discharged.

I make my way across the upper deck from the orangery, passing a closed swimming pool, a bar with the chairs up on the tables and a table-tennis table with the net missing. Normality is on its way for this particular cruise ship but it still has a way to go before the big beast glides around The Caribbean with passengers in brightly coloured shirts.

I thank all concerned and they deliver me back to dry land. I make my way to the carpark and climb aboard, feeling far more comfortable.

Day 69

Back on dry land where I belong and we're on our way once more after the mistake I made yesterday. It's not a million miles from here to Lulworth Cove, just a sedate drive this morning, but the memories will come flooding back at a much faster rate of knots when I get there. There's a stunning motor home campsite that awaits, overlooking the sea, and regardless of what time I arrive, I'm going to spend the day there and stay over as I have many times before in my past. I'm looking forward to it immensely.

Although called Lulworth Cove, the actual beach is called Man O'War Beach and that's where visitors will find Durdle Door.

I've made it. Lulworth Castle has a history, just like all other castles, but a very different kind of history to them. To reach the castle I drive through the strangely named village of Wool and make my way up the hill to Lulworth itself after a few nasty bends in the road.

The architect of the castle was the infamous Inigo Jones and work began on its building in 1588. Unlike most castles it has never seen conflict of any description as it was built as a hunting lodge, but in the style of a castle. The Weld Family have owned the estate for hundreds of years and that fact is where my memories begin.

I met Wilfred Weld through our associations with Hampshire Cricket Club and I was invited to perform here when he began hiring out the castle for corporate events. It worked really well. I seem to remember what impressed me most was the fact he had a pub, The Weld Arms, named after his family. Not many of us can boast that one.

The land from the castle falls away towards Lulworth Cove and the much-photographed Durdle Door, a big rock in the sea with a hole in the middle, which can be seen to the left. Long before I knew the Welds I came here on a family holiday and I snorkelled there for the first time in my life. I remember being told of the wonderful things I would see once my head was under the water, but, sadly, all I saw were my toes, a bit of a let-down really.

Durdle Door is regarded as the most popular Dorset structure with sightseers and its name derives from the old English word for drill. It's basically a limestone arch that has been affected by erosion, but hundreds of years ago, to help make it more of a tourist attraction, they called it The Dragon Drinking From The Sea. The sad thing about Durdle Door is that one day it will collapse and fall into the sea due to the weight above the famous arch. Mind you, it's 140 million years old so it probably won't fall down tomorrow. It's rotten luck if it does.

In more recent times I went back there when Wilfred decided to put music shows on in The Courtyard, by the entrance to the castle, adjacent to the cafeteria. It was a much smaller venue than the corporate events inside the ruins of the castle but I have to say, even being outdoors, it was a darn-sight warmer.

The sunset is sensational this evening as my eyes scan the horizon through the camper van's windscreen. To my right I can still see The Isle of Portland which I learnt so much about the other day and along the horizon, to my left, I see more land which I shall be visiting shortly. Wedged between Devon and

Hampshire I now realise what an underrated county Dorset is, so the time has come to settle down in the sleeping-bag with a good travel book that tells me more about this pearl on the south coast. Give me this moment rather than a cabin on a cruise ship any day

For starters, it's one of the very few counties in England that doesn't have a motorway running through it and that has to be a blessing. Oh, and it has the oldest post-box in Britain, dating back to 1853 and still in use today. How did posties deliver letters back then? Did they walk, ride a bike or horse? It's an interesting thought.

Compared to other counties it isn't that big, just 56 miles wide and 31 miles stretching inland. Obviously it's also a county, spelling-wise, that doesn't end with sex and, at my age, I have to say most of my days don't end with sex either so I feel somewhat as one with Dorset. I feel sleepy now so just a few more interesting facts before I fall asleep.

The Romans came here from the south by boat and from the east overland. With their arrival it became a strategic settlement area and many local skirmishes took place here. This final gem made my eyes even heavier. It was nothing new. I don't think there's a part of Britain I've been too on this trip that didn't suffer from The Romans turning up and throwing their weight about. I don't quite understand it all. They did all the good and bad stuff they did and then, for no accountable reason, they packed their bags and cleared off back to Italy. What was the point? I fully appreciate the merciless days of The British Empire have long gone, thankfully so, but I have learnt on this trip that we weren't the only ones who turned up uninvited and caused total chaos. This island we live on fell victim too, what with the Scandinavians and the Italians rushing at us from all directions. I sense that nowhere I have visited escaped the wrath of invaders but the only difference is that enemies of this island left behind some incredible monuments and wondrous architecture for the modern world to admire. Let's be honest, there wouldn't be Roman candles on bonfire night if they hadn't come here, so credit where it is due.

Right, that will do me for tonight.

Day 70

I say my farewells to The Weld Family and I'm on my way once more along the B3069 towards the village of Langton Matravers on The Isle of Purbeck. I've seen road-signs to this village many times but this is my first and very quick visit as I ensure my long journey stays as close to the coastline as possible.

I'm familiar with The Purbeck Folk Festival as many of my friends have performed at it, but I need to stop off at The Langton Matravers Museum in St George's Close to discover more and broaden my knowledge of the area.

My visit here is most fruitful as I have found out that Langton Matravers thrived through the quarries of limestone, also known as Purbeck marble, which was excavated in this vicinity 200 years ago. I love this kind of stuff, boring as it may seem to many.

The Isle of Purbeck is a peninsula that has very little access for motor vehicles. The English Channel is at its southernmost point and inland it's sort of detached from the mainland by The River Frome and Poole Harbour to its right. I say sort of detached because The River Frome is not big or strong enough to detach anything. Anyway, let's call it The Isle of Purbeck because everyone else does, though I do question its validity.

I sense the best way to get back to passable roads is to head up towards Wareham. I need to drive slightly inland as I make my way towards Wareham away from Ministry of Defence territory that is well and truly out of bounds. I'm not actually heading for Wareham today, it's just that I'm on the right road, but shortly I will turn right and drop down to Swanage. There is a road closer to the sea but a huge gate shows me I have no access, there is little choice but to take the road I'm permitted to take.

The whole area, either side of the road, looks like a holding area for Christmas trees, reminding me of the time I drove the long, straight road into Berlin in 1988. There's something quite dark and daunting about these kinds of military roads and, to be honest, I don't think I'd like to drive VW through them anyway, so I'm more than happy to take the alternative route, wherever it is. The whole area seems to be holding all kinds of sinister secrets, what with its threatening warning signs on high wire fences and red flags waving overhead. I am warned not to take any photographs. As if I would. Of all the places I've been to on this wonderful journey I think this is the most undesirable place I would want to take a photograph anyway. I'm fine thanks, I promise I won't interfere with your rules of disengagement.

It takes best part of an hour to escape this somewhat haunting experience as I drive through land that seems to have had bombs dropped on it. There are roads for military tanks too and I don't think I would have got away with VW passing as such a vehicle so I didn't even try. Surely all this military hardware could have kept The Romans at bay if they had tried harder? Just a thought. No, I'm not too impressed, but at least I know where to come if I need to steal a decent Christmas tree.

After such a somewhat haphazard drive today, weaving in and out of the impassable, I intend spending tomorrow evening in a far more laid-back manner at the delightful Mowlem Theatre on the seafront after exploring the town and its surrounding area during the day. They have a revue show on tomorrow night so I'm going to relax and enjoy myself for a few hours. A laugh, a song and a couple of beers will suit me fine, a nice end to whatever lays ahead tomorrow.

Day 71

So, my plan today is to drive around Swanage and its surrounding areas before heading around the coast to Poole tomorrow. The Danish fleet of warships once sailed to Swanage from a more watery direction than mine and Alfred The Great sank the lot of them, all 120 ships. Nice one Alfie. As I said, I'm approaching from a totally different direction so I reckon I'll be left alone.

I take the A351 to Corfe Castle, a small village 4 miles north of Swanage, which boasts one hell of a castle, despite the fact it's in ruins. I played an open-air concert there a few years ago and remember the grass mound surrounding the castle is about as steep as Mount Everest. My legs ached before I set foot on stage. It's now in the safe hands of The National Trust but during The English Civil War it was attacked twice, obviously by soldiers with equally weary legs. By all accounts it dates back to the 10ᵗʰ Century but, asking around, no-one seems to know why it ever was built in the first place. Maybe it was just because there happens to be a lot of stone around in this part of Britain and a few attacks would ensure the area didn't feel left out.

The population of Corfe Castle weren't a military-minded community though as most of them worked the land, providing raw clay for industry, rather than taking up arms and heading off to fighting.

Corfe Castle isn't very big but the road through it is like a snake. A sharp right turn beside the castle and then a sharp left as I leave the village and head off uphill towards Swanage.

It's a bit of a climb and poor old VW had to drop down to first gear at one point.

Hello Swanage. They didn't even have a road along its seafront until 1823 and so compared to other coastal towns it's a relatively new seaside attraction for tourists. Until then, like many other places within the area it mostly contributed to the quarrying industry. Those who didn't dig went fishing and, as far as Swanage is concerned, that was about it.

The Mowlem Theatre was the venue for my first performance after the 2021 lockdown and so it holds a very recent and very special place in my heart. It was wonderful to see a live audience after 17 months in the wilderness and I think the audience enjoyed the long-overdue liberation too. The view from the dressing room, across the sea, is quite unbelievable, a nice environment to tune up and get a show in the head. A gully runs alongside the stage-door and I spend time spotting little fish heading out into the unknown of The English Channel. Few will survive but I have no way of warning them.

I'm equally fascinated by The Swanage Railway. Actually, I am fascinated by old trains in general. I love steam trains and its great see a team of enthusiasts took on the challenge of re-opening the line after the famous railway cull of the 1960s and 70s when over 2,000 railway stations were closed and 5,000 miles of track were lost. Literally thousands of railway routes were closed- down as unviable. The aforementioned enthusiasts here bucked that trend and were having none of it. The line runs for just over 9 miles from Swanage to Wareham and it's a remarkable story of success. It isn't running today for some reason or I would be climbing on board like a shot. I accept steam trains don't help with the environment but they are amazing fetes of engineering. I'm sure more steam trains would have survived through the years had it not been for the invention of contact lenses, things that don't like little specks of dirt in the air.

I popped into the theatre to say hello and have a welcome cup of tea with the staff at The Mowlem who have invited me to the show this evening, a nice gesture and a welcome break. The only problem here is where to park the camper van. I decide to drive 2 miles out to Studland after the show, a bit out of the way, but at least I will touch the coast again before I make the 20-mile drive to Poole in the morning. What's at Studland? Well, there's 4 beaches, all owned by the National Trust. That's all I know. but it must be worth a visit.

Day 72

From my vantage point at Studland I can almost reach out and touch Bournemouth but I need to take the long way round via Poole as VW isn't an amphibious craft. There's a car ferry available but that would be cheating seeing as I can go there by road. Hey, if I want the easy option I could jump on one of those cruise ships I saw in Weymouth and sail round Britain. Where there is a road I always take it despite the easy options available.

Studland is a small village and Poole is a large town where I presume most Studlanders jump on the ferry for work and I'm about to see the difference as I make my way there.

To give you some idea of its size Poole Harbour is the largest natural harbour in the world and the town is a hell of a place to get to what with all the inlets, rivers and waterways that have congregated here.

I drive almost as far west as Lytchett Minster again and pick up the A35 that will set me in the direction of Poole, but I take a right fork towards Sterte, thus enabling me to stick to the water's edge. The town has numerous music venues, The Lighthouse is one of my favourites as it supports up and coming local acts in the area, an important incentive as there are few places for such musicians to learn their trade since lockdown. I seem to have been driving around this harbour for ages so it will be a relief to finally reach the town. I now see what they call it the largest harbour in the world.

Driving around a roundabout that may well be the biggest roundabout I've ever had to negotiate, well it has offices built on it, I follow the signs to the harbour. It's not the same as so many of the other harbours I've visited over the weeks, this is like some European marina and the road-signs are baffling to say the least. I've gone around the same roundabout three times and I'm still none the wiser.

Poole as a settlement goes back to The Iron Age and The Romans came here too, of course they did. They probably built this bloody roundabout.

The museum is situated in the Old Town in Lower High Street, and there's a boat there, made from the wood of a single oak tree, and it's estimated to be 2,000 years old. There's no real way of finding out as someone has stolen the engine. Amazing. It's a great thing to see before I'm mesmerised by the multitude of sailing craft in the harbour. It's like Monte Carlo without the Russian billionaires.

Carparking here in Poole is a complete nightmare and I search for over an hour for a suitable place for VW to rest up. To correct myself, there are ample carparking spaces, but they are all crammed to the hilt with cars that beat me to it. I've never been fond of multi-story parks for obvious security reasons and determined to keep my travel pal at ground level. I have an idea. I thought of taking the car-ferry across to Brownsea Island. But it turned out to be not such a great idea as there are no car-ferries to Brownsea Island. It's a shame because I had a hunch that the island would welcome all sorts of overnights seeing as a certain Baden-Powell set up an experimental camp there in 1907. It was a great success, the proof being that the scout movement was born. Not having ever been a boy scout I should have 'been prepared' and arrived in Poole much earlier before the traffic piled into the town and then I would have found somewhere to park, which in turn would have allowed me to visit Brownsea. Oh well.

I've been to Poole many times over the years, both the folk club and what was The Arts Centre and I've always enjoyed my visits, but this time it felt awkward. The drive around Britain has been relatively stress-free but I'm going to admit that I freaked out today. I was thinking about staying over tonight but I've now changed my mind and I'm heading out of town in an easterly direction. I seem to be following the signs for Ferndown.

Soon I shall be in Bournemouth, which, when I was young, happened to be in Hampshire, but they must have moved it because it's now in Dorset, which must mean that some smart-arse councillor got his or her hands on the plans and justified their job importance, so I don't really know where Bournemouth really is until I collide into it. If only I'd been a boy-scout. I could have used my compass.

Day 73

Ok then Bournemouth, where are you? Dorset or Hampshire, I'm searching for you.

The A35 here is wide and busy as it swings around numerous roundabouts and dives beneath underpasses at a rate of knots. This road is always blocked when the sun comes out. In fact, it's even blocked when the sun is threatening to come out, such is the lure of Bournemouth to those living inland. Today is cloudy as I approach the final week of my 80-day trip around Britain but there's still enough traffic on this road to make me keep my wits about me.

Before we head into the town centre I need to backtrack and head back west as I'd forgotten to drive around Sandbanks and pretend I'm a multi-millionaire. There's nothing wrong with dreaming and I'm about to dream.

Sandbanks is less than half a square mile and it's full of the most expensive houses in the country, many of which are owned by celebrities and top professional footballers. Far more interesting is the fact that John Lennon bought his beloved Aunt Mimi a house here and visited often.

I drive around the golden peninsula, which takes 12 minutes and then I leave. Most of the residents have never seen a vehicle as old as my VW camper van and they didn't take its arrival too well as they turned their noses up at it. VW felt like breaking down in the middle of road due to a filthy oil leak, but I managed to make it changed its mind. Even if I had the money to live on Sandbanks there's no way I'd tried in VW for a Bentley or a Rolls-Royce. VW is more than a camper van, it's my companion on the road and one that has never let me down.

Some things are way beyond value and my VW camper van happens to be one such thing.

Having said that, it was great to feel like a millionaire for 12 minutes, but now I must move on into the more normal part of the town before the HMRC get their claws into me, heaven forbid.

Oh yes, I've certainly performed in Bournemouth more times than I care to remember. My first time was at The Free Express Folk Club held at The Pembroke Arms in West Hill Road and I just have to take a drive-by for old time's sake. The pub is still here but the folk club has long gone.

Down at the beautiful beach there is The BIC, Bournemouth International Centre, a massive 4,000-seater where I supported Tom Jones, and directly across the road is The Pavilion where I did a season of my own Sunday night concerts in 1987. It's all changed now, way beyond recognition, what with pedestrian thoroughfares, fast-food places, gift shops and all that kind of thing, so I turn left, away from the sea, passing the Royal Bath Hotel where I stayed with great regularity, before joining the B3066 and the Bath Road where I hit an eternity of roundabouts. I re-join the A35 for just half a mile before dropping back down again to almost complete my full circle journey around this particularly busy, very commercialised part of the south coast. That read as complicated as the drive itself, for which I apologise.

Commercialised, noisy seaside resorts have never been my thing and I sadly lament the time when I could drive through Bournemouth, park outside The Pembroke Arms and leave my car there overnight if I'd consumed too much home-made wine. Do I miss those days? What do you think?

I knew enough about Bournemouth not to bother with a visit to The Tourist Information Centre, something that had become a regular thing over the last couple of months. Oh yes, and then there's my laziness as it's in the town centre where vehicles are forbidden and I don't fancy walking about in the rain that has fallen on the seaside resort, something rain does quite often on seaside towns. The tourist guides never mention that the one and only Tony Hancock lived here, a grave shortcoming I feel.

My musical connections with Bournemouth are, needless to say I'm sure, nothing compared to The Beatles who now crop up for the third time on my journey. They played here more times than anywhere else, other than Liverpool, between 1963 and 64. The With The Beatles album sleeve photo was taken at the Premier Inn in Westover Road when it was The Palace Court Hotel and George Harrison wrote his first song here, titled Don't Bother Me. I understand that lyric perfectly as I make my way out of Bournemouth towards Christchurch. It's all rather hectic through this town and I crave for the traffic here to thin out a little.

I'm spending the night at Three-Legged Cross before heading further east towards my starting point in Southampton. Why Three Legged Cross? It hosts my favourite car boot sale every Sunday and I go there often to find old, neglected musical instruments that I revitalise with acrylic landscape paintings, giving them a new lease of life and sense of purpose after being unceremoniously dumped by their previous owners, and we all remember that feeling don't we? Everything deserves a second chance and that includes musical instruments. Yes, I go in search of those old, neglected musical instruments and the chances are I may meet one or two old, neglected musicians too.

Staying in this lay-by, close to the car boot site, means I'll be at the front of the queue in the morning, which may help me pick up a few more musical bargains to store away in the wagon until I get back to Salisbury in a few days' time.

Day 74

It hasn't stopped raining all night and the car boot site seems to look in a sick and sorry state. There are just a few, hardy traders risking it today and none of them have any instruments for sale so I'm grabbing a quick coffee before moving on with no time to waste.

It isn't too far to Christchurch, about 7 or 8 miles and so I leave the field and toodle along at a leisurely pace. I have three good reasons to visit Christchurch today, two well defined and one not quite so obvious. Firstly, The Regent Theatre was where I was booked for two consecutive nights for the very first time in my career. Secondly, I once was asked to turn on their Christmas lights here and, just like today, it was pouring with rain and so hardly anyone turned up. In a similar way to today I sat and drank coffee, but in the chapel of an undertaker's premises, yes really. Thirdly, I once performed at a brilliant folk club here, but it was nearly 50 years ago and I can't for the life of me remember the name of the pub where it was held.

I'm hoping my drive here will reignite some of my memory cells and take me to that distant, hazy venue. I usually have a good memory for such old gigs, but this one just won't come into my head.

Returning to the coast road I came here via the A338 passing through some delightfully unspoilt areas mixed in with the built-up places such as Boscombe and Southbourne. Christchurch is sort of inland but it isn't. It's protected by a large peninsula, Christchurch Harbour, where Mudeford provides the only real form of human life from what I've seen.

I should point out we're talking about Christchurch in England here and not the more famous Christchurch in New Zealand. That would have meant I definitely took the wrong turning somewhere. Hey, you have to be somewhere special if they steal your name on the other side of the world.

Christchurch is situated where the Rivers Avon and Dorset Stour converge upon the harbour inlet. There was a time when it had a thriving fishing industry until boats began to be built bigger and the harbour became too shallow to cater for them. At that point many of the locals turned to smuggling and Christchurch became one of the most prolific smuggling locations in Britain. Maybe that's how the early settlers on Sandbanks managed to buy such big houses.

It's a beautiful drive around the various waterways and it isn't difficult to work out why Christchurch is high on the rankings as a retirement area with over a third of its population over retirement age. And to think I mocked Worthing when I started out over 2 months ago. This place takes the biscuit, dunked in a lukewarm cup of tea of course, but it takes the biscuit anyway.

Unable to find the folk club pub I came here to see, either in my head or on the road, I leave Christchurch by the coastal road that hugs the north of the harbour and I make my way towards Friars Cliff and eventually Highcliffe Castle.

Situated in Rothesay Drive, Highcliffe Castle isn't a castle in the usual sense as it wasn't built until 1831 but interesting it certainly is and well worth the drive because it is so grand. So who moved here in 1916? None other than Harry Gordon Selfridge and his wife. I know this story well as I composed the music for a documentary about this shop owner, second only in retail fame to Charles Harrod.

The couple lived here for 6 years and whilst here Rose, being American, set up a convalescence area for American soldiers wounded overseas during World War 1.

The really sad end to the documentary, which involved me composing sombre music as a finale, was that, in 1947, Harry Gordon Selfridge died in poverty in London, but his body was brought back here from a pauper's grave to be buried in St Marks Churchyard next to Rose. I had to drive here and pay my respects due to my musical involvement with his sad story. From rags to riches and back to rags sums up the life of Mr Selfridge, a huge name, yet a man who built up huge debts.

I'm heading to Barton on Sea next where I shall bed down for the night before entering the county of Hampshire tomorrow. I hope you agree that there isn't a county in Britain I have visited on this journey that hasn't produced something of real interest, but I think the most surprising has been Dorset. In my head it's no longer wedged between Devon and Hampshire, but a county that can boast more history than most.

Day 75

So, this morning we say goodbye to Dorset and all its hidden secrets and say hello to Hampshire, our journey nearly done.

Today there is a twist in the tail and we need to travel a little faster than usual if we are to reach Lymington, on the southern edge of The New Forest in time to spring a surprise for you. That's where we catch the afternoon ferry to The Isle of Wight. Well, I didn't exclude some of the islands on the west coast of Scotland and now I must not do the same down on the south coast too. I even thought about setting off to The Channel Islands from Poole until I realised they aren't part of The United Kingdom. To be honest, I didn't realise The Isle of Man wasn't either, but every day is a school day. The Isle of Wight is different though, so we're heading there right now. It's definitely part of England and so we're bending the rules a little today as we sail off to take a look.

The road distance around The Isle of Wight is nearly 70 miles and so the plan is to take the VW camper van over there for 2 days, similar to the Scottish adventure, as I re-visit some lovely theatres on the island. But first we must drive to Lymington, a short drive of 9 miles.

Lymington is as posh as Poole and there are so many yachts and motor cruisers here that it seems as though it's compulsory to own one if you live here. There are three different marinas here and it's a popular trip to the coast for those visiting The New Forest. I have a feeling it's actually classed as part of The New Forest.

The dock to the south-east of the town is where I drive VW onto the ferry, Wight Sun. It's a straight voyage south across The Solent to Yarmouth and it doesn't take more than an hour to get there. There's been a ferry service here for nearly 200 years.

There are so many boats on The Solent, a bit like a marine rush-hour as they all fly about in different directions. Mind you, they all seem to have the sense to get out of the way of this thing. It's bigger than all the rest of them and it's travelling in a straight line, no messing. They say wind rules over engines but it doesn't look much like that to me.

The famous Needles are on our right, on the edge of the island, as we edge slowly into Yarmouth. I leave the ferry to begin my anti-clockwise drive around the island on the A3054, which will start with a tiny bridge that takes us over the estuary. But first things first, lunch.

One of my favourite restaurants, Salty's, in Quay Street, is within walking distance of the ferry carpark and fish served here couldn't be fresher. They have an upstairs area that can be booked for private functions and that's how I originally discovered the place a good few years ago when I was booked to perform at a corporate event. I fell in love with the restaurant and it's a delight to return here today to enjoy a sea bass with French salad, the poshest and most substantial meal the Weymouth cruise ship.

And so, with a full stomach, my journey around the island begins. As I drive towards The Needles, in the VW this time, let me tell you a little about the island.

The Romans stayed on the island for 400 years, maybe due to the lack of ferries that would take them off, maybe not, and due to its position in The English Channel it has always been a vulnerable target for marauding navies, including The Spanish Armada.

In 1970 the island was invaded by half a million different types who came here for the first Isle of Wight Festival, headlined by Jimi Hendrix. It took place at Afton Down, to the west of the island, and will probably go down in history second only to Woodstock, so much so that in 2006 they erected a statue of the great guitarist at Dimbola Lodge. They didn't hold another festival here for over 30 years when Robert Plant of Led Zeppelin headlined. Oh yes, they all played here, from Bruce Springsteen to The Rolling Stones and so it was no big deal Richard Digance performed on the island, which he did many times. The island had its fair share of folk clubs, the most successful being at Wootton Bridge, and I reckon I performed at most of them before I made it to the concert stages of the bigger theatres.

I first performed here in concert at The Sandown Pavilion, then at The Medina Theatre in Newport, an inland venue on the B3399 and therefore out of bounds, and more recently in Ventnor and the holiday village in Bembridge. I take tea at The George Hotel, directly opposite the Sandown gig on the end of a short pier and recall how it must be the first time I came and didn't leave with a stinking hangover.

I stay on the A3055 as I make my way along the bottom of the island from Freshwater all the way across to Ventnor, a ragged journey of 19 miles. On this south-west point of the island I take up my overnight position, staring out at the numerous commercial tankers from other lands that hang out here so they don't have to pay mooring fees at Southampton. It reminds me of a few weeks ago when I heard about all the cruise ships that were lined up in hospital off Weymouth, waiting to be given the clean bill of health, green light to get on with their business. It's quite eerie to see them lit up at night, bobbing about in complete silence whilst they avoid having to pay rent.

Day 76

Yesterday I drove around two-thirds of the Isle of Wight in an anti-clockwise direction so today I edge along the east coast of the island before heading west back towards Yarmouth and my return voyage to Lymington.

Hanging off the east coast are towns including Shanklin, Sandown and Bembridge, towns battered by the winds off the sea. At Sandown I leave the A3055 to explore the small coastal roads to Bembridge at the island's west-most tip, before turning west towards Seaview and Ryde. We're not too far from where The Mary Rose sank.

They built a pier in Ryde in 1814, the 4th longest pier in Britain, the reason being the levels of the tides. Before the pier the ferries would arrive here and the passengers would disembark and be carried over half a mile in a horse and cart to dry land.

More coast road from Ryde to Fishbourne and then on to East Cowes, probably the island's most famous town as it's the centre of all kinds of sailing events. There's a ferry here too that could take me back to the mainland but it's out of the question as I would miss out on more Hampshire coastline if I did so. Because of this I drive through East Cowes, all way down the estuary and then back up again to West Cowes. I know very little about sailing other than the fact it's a great way of using old sheets from your bed, but I'm right in the hub of such an activity. Everyone seems to wear Crew jumpers and blue deck shoes with white trim around here. It's a kind of uniform that says you have every right to be here and it makes me realise, due to my ignorance, that I have no right whatsoever to be here.

Once again I could take the A320 into Newport and take the easy route but I choose to keep to the coast towards Gurnard as I make my way back to Yarmouth. To my right I can see the mainland of Southampton and then Bournemouth in the distance as I make my way west.

There are all sorts of fortifications to be seen along The Solent from The Isle of Wight, hardly surprising when you think of its geographical threat from enemy fleets through the years. Calshot Castle is now in view, a castle built by King Henry V111 as a proof he did things other than marry and divorce women. He was quite active along The Solent with his ships and fortifications. Well, let's be honest he was quite active anywhere in so many ways.

I have so enjoyed my drive around The Isle of Wight as it has brought back so many musical memories. I never came here as a child and so such memories are relatively new but they are just as special. The music pubs and concert halls have given me memories on an island I don't visit very often and yet adding them all up I reckon I must have played 20 times in my career. My only regret as I say goodbye to the island is that I never saw Bob Dylan here, or any of the other great musicians that came and performed here. Well you never know, Dylan may just be sitting in the passenger lounge on the ferry back to Lymington.

As I head back to the mainland a most peculiar feeling comes into my head as I see places I have visited to the left and Southampton, where it all ends, to the right. It reminds that my 80-day trip around Britain is almost over and it brings a tinge of sadness to my mind. It all seems so long ago when I started out, but I can't get too emotional as I haven't completed the journey yet. There's one very special place I wish to add to my list of visits, but first of all I need to get back on the mainland, now only half an hour away. A few blasts to let the smaller boats know we're on our way stir from my thoughts and suddenly I'm back on the job, concentrating on getting VW off the ferry without any chassis damage.

Day 77

Back on the mainland there is a sense of excitement within me as I prepare to visit my favourite place in the whole of Britain, Bucklers Hard. You will hear why very shortly, but for now I wait in the queue to alight from the ferry and make my way through Lymington once more. My next destination isn't too far, just 9 miles.

Ok, before we explore Bucklers Hard, and I can't wait, we drive 2 miles north, to the motor museum of Lord Montagu of Beaulieu. It has to be done. If you think my VW camper van is an old relic then it's nothing in age compared with what's on show here. VW is feeling like a teenager as we both stare at the cars on display. Anyway I made the diversion for VW and not us so now we drive on to Bucklers Hard.

You may recall that I named Polperro as my favourite place in Britain a few days ago whilst we were in Cornwall. Well, that may well be the case but Bucklers Hard is by far and way my favourite place when it comes to historical interest, and you're about to find out why.

This is a truly amazing place if you like your British history as much as I do. It's nothing more than a cluster of Georgian cottages by the Beaulieu River, but that's one hell of an under-sell.

I stand here in wonder as my imagination runs riot. Imagine this, a huge pile of logs arrives from The New Forest by horse-drawn carts and they're placed by the cottages at the top of the hill. That is when the work begins because the cottages are occupied by various craftsmen who go about their work as the forest logs transform into giant sailing ships as they get

268

closer and closer to the water's edge. Such invention, such a hive of industry, around just a couple of dozen cottages that played a major part in building Britain's navy.

So what did they build here? In 60 years from those logs they built 43 warships for The British Navy including 3 that fought at The Battle of Trafalgar, alongside Horatio Nelson in 1805. They were by name, Euryalus, Agamemnon and Swiftsure. Now that's what I call history in all its glory.

When Sir Francis Chichester became the first man to sail around the world single-handedly in Gypsy Moth, he also set off from and returned to Bucklers Hard, adding more history to this incredible place.

As I take a last stroll down the hill before returning to the camper van, there's a special cottage, 82 High Street, round about halfway down on the left. It's a church. Yes, one of the tiny worker's cottages is a real church called St Mary's Chapel, about the size of a large living room, and it's still operative to this day for off-the-wall weddings. Originally it was a little school for the children of the craftsmen until they converted it into a chapel in the 19th Century. You have to know it's there or you walk straight past it with not so much as a second glance.

Now you understand why I had to bring the camper van here and why it's my favourite place in Britain. It just oozes history and my drive around our coastline would not have been complete had we not come here today.

Is there my usual musical connection to Bucklers Hard? Not really other than the fact that a former member of Dire Straits runs a pub just down the road, but that's about it. Let's just say that the thought of going to Bucklers Hard today was music to my ears and that's good enough for me.

A wonderful day draws to a close as I enjoy a pot of tea and custard tart in the tiny café by the carpark. My journey continues through the southern part of The New Forest, another interesting outpost, but that can wait until tomorrow as I want to stay here as long as I possibly can. It's against the rules but I've been given special dispensation to stay overnight and take in my final breaths of the amazing Bucklers Hard. I've been here so many time the staff here know me and when I tell them of my journey around Britain in 80 days they extend an invitation to me to rest up for the night in their carpark, for which I am most grateful. From here I spy Cowes on the other side of The Solent and it, strangely, seems a long time ago that I was making my way around The Isle of Wight looking in this direction from over there.

Day 78

The New Forest is unique, there's no other part of Britain like it and the drive up from Bucklers Hard is a peaceful journey, avoiding the ponies that stroll around, thinking they own the place, which of course they do, thanks once again to Henry V111. I pass Hythe and Marchwood to my right as I head back up north towards my final destination, my return to Southampton.

If you recall, I mentioned yesterday that this is where the logs came from for the building of the warships at Bucklers Hard and it was proclaimed a Royal Forest by William The Conqueror in 1079. This didn't make him a kind, giving man of the common people, far from it. The forest was claimed as a hunting ground for the upper-classes and animals were allowed to reside there on the condition they could be hunted by the wealthy. For that reason he filled the land with unfortunate deer to allow him to enjoy his bloodthirsty pursuits. The more I learn of William The Conqueror the more I dislike him. If Harold hadn't been shot in the eye at The Battle of Hastings he would never have his evil way once he'd taken control.

Folklore states that William was a devil for charging land rent and rights to his so-called landowners and he sent gangs of thugs around to collect the monies owed, thus the term paying the Bill. I wonder if that's true.

The New Forest is 150 square miles of unspoilt land that very oddly doesn't look anything like the land that surrounds it. Why, I have no idea. If anything it looks like it belongs in Scotland rather than England, what with its scrubland and wildness. This part of the forest runs along the western side of the estuary into Southampton from The Solent and isn't as densely populated as the eastern side, thus the sedate journey today. The New Forest gained National Park status in 2005 and quite a few luminaries have settled here, including Sherlock Holmes author, Sir Arthur Conan Doyle and Florence Nightingale whom we shall pay our respects to tomorrow, a fitting thing to do as she was the first woman of nursing and we all know how thankful we are to such hard-working nurses who helped to get us through the last few years of global despair.

Day 79

The penultimate day of our journey, Day 79, and I have purposefully chosen a very special visit to the village of Wellow before I end up back in Southampton tomorrow as my final destination. I have lived in this area for many years now and St Margaret's Church has always had a special place in my heart. I hope it will shortly have a special place in your heart too.

Considering how many lives our front-line workers saved during 2020 and 2021 I am proud to hold a torch to the woman who developed nursing during The Crimean War, Florence Nightingale. She is quite possibly the only woman, outside of royalty, who is known solely by her Christian name.

Florence became a national hero and saved so many lives on the battlefield, so much so that when she died they wanted to give her a London funeral and a final resting place in Westminster Abbey, as suggested by Queen Victoria, but she had demanded, before she left us, that she should be laid to rest beside her parents, peacefully and out of the public eye in St Margaret's Church, Wellow, near Romsey in Hampshire.

It's hard to find the church without a little help and many potential visitors fail, but for those who do make it they are truly humbled by the pure white memorial that stands in the tiny graveyard behind the church. The initials FN on the monument say all that needs to be said. How to find Florence's final resting place? It's a short drive north up the A36 signposted to Salisbury before turning right at Winwhistle Road at the top of the hill. Just a mile to the left is the tiniest of lanes. There is a partly hidden sign for St Margaret's Church but that's equally tiny and thus easy to miss.

It's ironic that the bi-centennial recognition of Florence Nightingale's birth coincided with the start of the dreaded intruder to our lives. 200 years apart and yet bound together by Florence's pioneering work in nursing. Because of this I trust you shall forgive the indulgence of a diversion 8 miles inland and I hope you agree this had to be done. It also gives me a chance to take lunch at my local pub before I begin my final day.

To say they've put the flags out is an understatement and a couple of close friends have given VW, my VW camper van, a once over so that it looks beautiful upon its return to Southampton tomorrow. In many different ways this has been such a wonderful and thoughtful penultimate day. The journey has been a multitude of personal memories. So many friends I have lost along the way have been remembered over the last 80 days but now I must put away the sadder memories as I prepare for a day of total celebration tomorrow. I often wondered if both myself and my four-wheeled companion would stay the course but stay the course we most certainly did. So put the flags out Southampton, we're on our way.

So many of my friends here are suggesting we should pop a cork and enjoy a nice glass of champagne but I decline because the job isn't quite done. I'll be driving tomorrow so it isn't a great idea anyway but, additionally, the celebration is when you win the cup, not when you just reach the final. So instead of a liquid celebration I sit down this evening with friends and enjoy a lovely meal as I tell them all about the theatres I have re-visited, the memories that each part of Britain re-kindled and things I shared with you along the way.

I've been offered numerous places to stay tonight but I decline all the kind offers because I must spend the last night of my trip around Britain in my VW camper van. How could I possibly leave it stranded on the eve of such an achievement? Of course I couldn't and you wouldn't either. I've spent many evenings in this, my local pub, but this is the first time I have ever spent a night here in the carpark.

Day 80

We made it, me and VW. We were both so excited as we drove the final 12 miles towards our starting point.

My final destination is the ferry terminal in Southampton, adjacent to the very spot where The Titanic set sail and I see the dock gate in the distance as I drive along the A33, on West Quay Road, to come to rest at The Isle of Wight terminal. There are cruise ships moored to my right, proof they really are back in business after such a long lay-off.

I would estimate our journey took in around 6 thousand miles around the coastline of Britain and now we are back safe and sound. I give full credit to the camper van as I can't see too many vehicles being assembled today that will survive a similar journey in 30 years' time.

Is it an anti-climax to have completed the trip? Not at all. I'm a proud person today and I hope you enjoyed coming on such a magical journey with me. There are so many hidden treasures around our island and I loved both re-visiting old places and discovering new facts about places I hadn't been to before.

I met with old friends and made many new friends too as I realised the dream of something I'd always wanted to do. I think in total I've mentioned around 250 venues that have allowed me to have such a wonderful musical career and I enjoyed waving a big thank you to so many of them on my journey.

I trust my contributors have enjoyed their own particular memories too as they made their way to their own special parts of Britain's coastline.

What's next? I may try swimming The English Channel longways or walk around the planet to find out if I would be upside down when I reach the South Pole. We shall see, but for now I shall take my leave and put the camper van in for a well-deserved service. Thank you so much for coming along with me. Could I go round a second time now I'm back in Southampton? Absolutely no chance.

The Conclusion

So you see, my journey was nothing like a Bill Bryson kind of trip around Britain. I told you so at the very beginning did I not. I also told you my 80-day adventure would be nothing like that undertaken by Jules Verne when he went around the world in the same number of days. I told you that too.

So to conclude, my drive around Britain was just short of 7,000 miles in the end. At 35 miles to the gallon my trusty camper van drank exactly 200 gallons of fuel. The most incredible thing is that 200 gallons would have cost just £100 when VW came off the assembly line. Imagine that, going round the entire coastline of Britain in 80 days for just £100. If only. The cost in today's money has been just over £1,000. I should have done this journey 50 years ago and saved myself some money. Oh, and let's add £200 for the new tyre.

According to my notes I've re-visited or mentioned approximately 300 theatres and 250 pubs where I performed over half a century. I became a professional musician at the age of 18, that was 54 years ago. With my dubious skills of simple arithmetic I've worked out that I've been rather busy entertaining the public because the venues visited only represent just a small percentage of performances throughout my career. Even so, this adventure has brought back memories that I never thought would re-surface.

Having said all of that there is one very special thing about this journey that I am particularly proud of. It has nothing to do with performances through the years but more the fact that I have driven nearly 7,000 miles over 80 days and I didn't drive a single mile on a motorway, not a single mile. I think that's something to feel really proud about. I hate motorways and I've driven 1,000s and then more 1,000s of miles on the horrible things over the years. I've been done for speeding a few times, picked up more points than a crap football team and suffered a few minor bumps and thumps along the way. I had no intention of bringing such driving into my magical adventure. Poor old VW couldn't have been done for speeding if it had tried and we stayed clear of all other vehicles, or it may be more accurate to say other vehicles stayed clear of us.

I smile at the thought of the tens of thousands of cars that overtook us over the last 80 days, none of them having the foggiest idea what I was doing or where I was going. I bet they would have been so envious if they had known. Most of them were probably going backwards and forwards to work or appointments and I wonder what they would have given to swap places with me, to travel the beautiful coastline of Britain. The big problem is that I wouldn't have swapped with them for all the rocks around Scotland.

It's been a fantastic experience and I hope you enjoyed coming along with me.

Printed in Great Britain
by Amazon

75451681R00159